Abba Daddy Do

exploration s in child like faith

by Dr. Jacob Youmans
illustrated by Maile & Leilani Youmans

III TRI-PILLAR PUBLISHING

Tri-Pillar Publishing
Anaheim Hills, California
Website: www.TriPillarPublishing.com
e-mail: tripillarpublishing@cox.net

International Standard Book Number --13:   978-0-9818923-4-4

International Standard Book Number --10:   0-9818923-4-5

Library of Congress Control Number: 2011940089

First edition, October, 2011

Printed in the United States of America

Contents

Acknowledgments   5

Foreword   7

Introduction   11

Fall   19
    Build a Bear   21
    Hide and Seek   25
    Walking   29
    Friends   33
    The Truth   37
    Dress-Up   43
    When You Get It, You Go   49
    The Offering   55
    Pray Like a Child   59
    Thank You!   63

Winter   69
    Important Work   71
    Patience   75
    Even More than Daddy   79
    Christmas Presents   83
    A New Year   87
    Happy   91
    Missing   95
    What Do You Do?   99
    Spending Time with Daddy   103
    Confession   107

Contents *(continued)*

Spring   113

    Play Ball!   115

    The Scooter   119

    Heartbreak   125

    Hurry!   131

    Hiding and Hunting   135

    Separation   139

    Carry Me   143

    Career Day   147

    What Does Daddy Do?   151

    Blessing   155

Summer   161

    The Hike   163

    The Cricket   167

    The Road Trip   171

    Measuring Up   177

    The Soak Zone   183

    Eye on the Ball   187

    Whom Do We Cheer For?   191

    Lost!   197

    The Chair   201

    The Gold Medal   205

Acknowledgments

First and foremost, I have to thank God – our Heavenly Father. It may seem overly simplistic to say that I have learned more about Him as Father through the adventure of raising children, but it's undoubtedly true. Thank You God for the gift of families and for calling us into Your family!

I need to thank my parents and grandparents for showing me so many different sides of parenting. You all taught me the power of adventure and made sure my childhood was never boring.

My editors, Josephine and Andy Dibble – thank you for always believing in me and in these simple stories! You are incredible alchemists yet again as you have turned lead into gold with this book! Thank you so much!

Peter Dibble – the cover design is awesome!

Daniel DeHoyos, Caitlin Hanna, Ross Owens, and Michael Pieper – I have been truly blessed to have you as students and to call you my friends! Thank you so much for the help you gave to this project. Your contributions to the prayers, questions, and suggested activities liven up this book more than you'll ever know. I'm so excited to see how God's going to use you in your lives and ministries!

To my ridiculously amazing wife Christy – it's safe to say on multiple levels that there would be no *Abba Daddy Do* without you! You are the greatest mother on earth – I learn so much from watching you every day. I love you so much and look forward to someday – long from now – working on *Abba Granddaddy Do* with you!

Maile and Leilani – you are the most difficult when it comes to writing "acknowledgments." Obviously, you play a major role in this book. The book wouldn't exist without you! I know you will read this book to all of your friends, to all of our family members, to all of your teachers and mentors, to your future husbands, and someday to your very own children. This is something you will read, and hear my voice in your head, long after I have gone on to heaven. So it's got to be really, really good...

Girls: don't ever lose your childlike faith. Read over the forewords you wrote again and again – you exude childlike faith in everything that you do. I am so proud of you and love you so much! But most importantly, never forget that as much as I love you, Jesus loves you so much more! Girls, I have dreams for you, but they are nothing compared to the dreams God has for you! I am excited to watch you grow into the young ladies and women that God has dreamed you to be! Oh – and please always call me "Daddy." That's my favorite title in the world!

God – Father, Son, and Holy Spirit – bless this book and remind us all of the beauty and simplicity of childlike faith! Guide us on the adventure now and forever – AMEN!

Foreword

 Hi, my name is Maile Youmans. I love this book so much, and I hope you enjoy it too! I'm so excited for this book – it has lots of memories of Leilani and me. I love all of the stories. I really think you'll enjoy it.

I love my family so much because they take care of me and make me happy. My family is nice. My sister plays with me all the time and is so much fun.

And I love Jesus so much because He gave me a great mom, dad, and sister. I love Jesus because He died for our sins.

Our favorite baseball team is the Dodgers as you can see on the back of the book. I like them because my dad likes them. One time we went to a Dodgers baseball game. It was so much fun, but then the Dodgers lost. It was a close game, but when it was over Leilani said, "Oh man – we came here for nothing!" But I think we didn't go there for nothing because it was still a lot of fun to be together as a family.

We always play games. I love games, and I always win! I love playing golf and tennis. They are such fun games, and games we can do as a family.

I wrote a book before called *The Magic Flower*. I turned it into a play at home too.

I love school and I love all of my teachers. We have lots of fun activities at school, and my favorite subjects are science and math.

Hope you enjoy this book!

Maile Youmans, age 8

. . . . .

Hi, my name is Leilani. I love my Daddy's books and I love Jesus! I love this book because I love my dad! This book makes me feel like I have great adventures. This book is about Maile's and my adventures. We love to play with each other and our Daddy.

I love Jesus more than anyone because He died on the cross for my sins. Jesus loves me no matter what, and so does my dad. But Jesus loves me more.

One time I got lost at the movie theater. We were watching the movie *Kung Fu Panda*. I had to go to the bathroom. So my dad had to leave the movie with me. My dad was done before me, so he went into the hall. I was still finishing. When I was done, I couldn't find my dad. But my dad was watching me the whole time. Then finally we got to watch *Kung Fu Panda* together again.

One time we had to go to sleep. My sister had a dream that I got lost. So she woke Dad up and told him. He searched everywhere – except for on my bed. Then he finally looked there and I was fast asleep. So was my sister.

One of my favorite times with my dad is when we go golfing. It's special because we both like it. It's fun and I always win – and my dad always loses. My dad and I love to play games with each other, and my dad always loses and I always win.

I hope you like this book. My dad wrote this book just for me and my sister – but also so people can learn about Jesus. I hope you learn that Jesus loves you no matter what!

Love,

Leilani Youmans, age 6… and a half

Introduction

"Abba Daddy Do!" It's kind of fun to say, but what does this mean? No, it's not the phrase Fred Flintstone yells at the end of every workday as he slides down the dinosaur's tail in *The Flintstones.* I do, however, have many fond childhood memories of watching Saturday morning cartoons with my dad. Saturday mornings were a special time.

And "Abba" has nothing to do with ABBA, the super-popular Swedish pop group. To be honest, I'm not a fan at all – sorry. In fact, when *Dancing Queen* is played during wedding receptions, I usually leave the dance floor. That is, if I'm even on the dance floor to begin with...

"Abba" is the Hebrew word for "Daddy." It's a more playful and intimate word for Father. It's the root word of the name of the great Hebrew Patriarch Abraham, whose name roughly translates to "Big Daddy." God promised Abram that he would be a father of many, many people – as many as there are stars in the sky (Genesis 15:4-6) and grains of sand on the seashore (Genesis 22:17), and part of His promise involved a name change to "Big Daddy" (Genesis 17:1-8). And boy – did God keep His promise, as He always does!

Jesus Himself uses the word "Abba" in a prayer in Mark 14:36. But this isn't just any prayer – it's one of His last prayers on earth. He's in the Garden of Gethsemane before His arrest and crucifixion. In this prayer, He is asking God for a "Plan B" because "Plan A" involves going through the brutal torture of the cross, and He'd prefer not to. He'd love a Plan B – but there isn't one. So He fulfills Plan A, because of His incredible love for you and for me. It's perhaps one of the most important prayers of Jesus' life – and our eternal life – and He chose to use the word "Abba."

St. Paul also uses the word "Abba" in the book of Romans and the book of Galatians (8:15 and 4:6, respectively). Both passages show the intimacy God desires to have with His people. God is love – Abba is love!

Now, "Daddy Do" was the first complete sentence my oldest daughter Maile ever uttered... and she still says it frequently. Sometimes I do it – whatever "it" is – and sometimes I don't. Instead, I sometimes strive to: allow, convince, encourage, motivate, inspire, demand or force her to do it. How else will she grow? We learn the most by doing – not by having it done for us.

But "Daddy Do" is also about the idea that our heavenly Father did "it" for us. He created us. He sent His one and only Son Jesus to live the perfect life for us – and to die a brutal death that we deserve. And He rose by His own power to conquer sin. And Jesus sent us the promised Holy Spirit, the power of God who lives in us and works through us. God did it!

This book is NOT a "father knows best" book. Often times it's a "father knows least" book, or at least an "earthly-father knows least" book. Sure, I might be able to get a little fatherly wisdom in there every now and then, but mostly it's about how and what I learn about life and faith from the "child-ness" of my daughters. If you're looking for a book where the father's a hero, put this book down. I'm just along for the adventure. But what is the adventure?

In the first three books of the New Testament, Matthew, Mark, and Luke, Jesus tells us about childlike faith. He says that to enter the kingdom of heaven, we must become like a little child. In Matthew 18, the disciples ask Jesus who's the greatest in the kingdom of heaven. (I'm sure each one of them secretly hoped that Jesus was going to say they were.) Jesus tells them, and all of us, that the greatest is the one who takes a position like a little child (Matthew 18:4). In John 3 (the same chapter that gives us John 3:16 – the "gospel in a nutshell") Jesus is having a conversation with Nicodemus. Nicodemus is a Pharisee and respected as one of the wisest men in all of Israel. He too is asking about the kingdom of heaven and how one can receive it, and Jesus tells him that to inherit the kingdom of God he must be "born again." He must become like the littlest of children. This childlike faith concept comes up again and again in the ministry of Jesus.

That's what this book is about – the adventure of childlike faith – looking at the world with childlike eyes and experiencing Jesus with childlike love and trust. For a child, everything's new and exciting, everything's magical, full of mystery and wonder. Things can be big and scary – but through it all, childlike faith knows that Abba Daddy is there. Fathers are so important.

· · · · ·

And as a father, let me introduce my family…

First and foremost, there is Christy, a.k.a., "Mommy." We got married June 20th, 1998, in Las Vegas. (It was in a church – and, no, Elvis was not my best man!) She is truly the love of my life and my best friend. We have been in ministry together our entire relationship, which means our life is in the "fishbowl" – everybody's watching. In fact, I proposed to her

April 8th, 1997, while leading a typical high school Bible study on love and relationships. This was very intentional because I wanted her to know that if she said "yes" (she did!), this was going to be our lives – played out for everyone to see, watch, observe, and critique. We take being role models as a couple and as a family very seriously.

To get back at me, Christy told me we were pregnant with our firstborn during the announcement time of our Youth Worship experience in front of hundreds of people. She won! The church gave us a literal standing ovation – and I was left absolutely speechless – which is pretty hard to do!

Maile, our first child, was born in June, 2003. She was due at the end of May, and with the name Maile Ann Youmans we gave her the initials M.A.Y., thinking it would be a fun way to remember her birth month. But then she was born in June! I'll never forget holding her for the first time. She was the most beautiful thing in the universe, and as I held her I really had only one thought – "I have no idea what I'm doing!"

Meanings of names are important to Christy and I, and we gave Maile her name because in Hawaiian it means "special blessing." And has she ever lived up to her name! In fact, I'll go out on a limb and say she's been our *very* special blessing! At the publishing of this book, she's in third grade.

A year and a half after Maile was born came Leilani. Christy "told" me she was pregnant with Leilani by putting the pregnancy test on my pillow as I came home late from a Dodgers baseball game. I woke her up and hugged and kissed her – and then realized that she had peed on that test – and it was now on my pillow! Leilani is Hawaiian for "heavenly flower," and again it's been a very fitting name. Leilani's beautiful, inside and out. At the publishing of this book, she's six and a half. (And when you're only six, the "half" is a big deal!)

As you will see throughout these stories, Maile and Leilani are sometimes best friends and sometimes worst enemies. They have much in common, and at the same time they are very different. But the thing that impresses me the most about both of them is their incredible faith, joy, and love of life. I am so proud to be their Daddy. I am an imperfect father to say the least, but it's a role I take very seriously and absolutely adore. I know that they are watching everything, and how I treat their mother is how they will expect to be treated by their future husbands. And how I treat them is not only how they will expect their husbands to treat their children, but it also gives them a glimpse of their heavenly Father. This is truly a responsibility I cannot take lightly.

· · · · ·

Before we get too far, I need to give a message to fathers. Look at the picture on the following page. It's Maile's first family portrait from her three-year-old preschool class. To me, this is a priceless work of art! But there are some things I want you to pay special attention to. The three smaller people at the top are Mommy, Maile, and Leilani. Notice how happy they are. Notice how they are holding hands. But now notice the big person at the bottom. That's me. That's Daddy. Notice how Daddy's not so happy. Notice how Daddy's away from the rest of the family. Daddy is the biggest – almost bigger than everyone else combined – but he's not at all engaged with the rest of the family.

This is the perception that three-year-old Maile had of our family! I had been traveling quite a bit at this point in her life, and I had been stressed out with complications at work and in

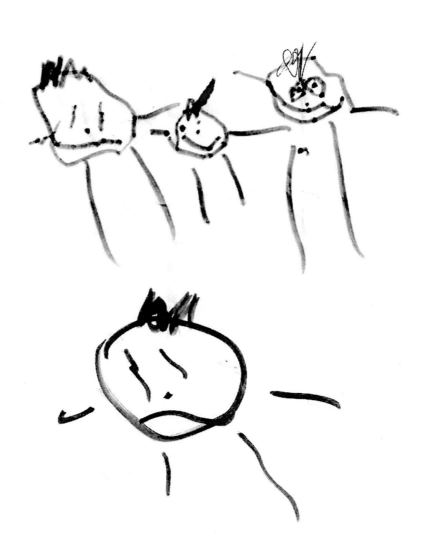

life generally, but this picture gives me goose bumps every time I look at it to this day – and I'm certain it always will.

I don't want this to be my family! I want us all to hold hands and be happy! But I have to more than "want" it. I have to do it. I have to work at it. I have to make my family my top priority. I can't just say it – I have to *live* it. It does not mean the travel and stress go away. In fact, I travel more often and have even more stress now than ever before. But it's a matter of really being there when I *am* there. This picture will always be a reminder to me of priorities. Children have so much to teach us!

Like all good adventures, childlike faith is not easy. But where's the fun in easy? I constantly tell my students: "You don't want life to be easy. Easy is boring." And following Jesus with childlike faith is never boring... or easy! This is all about a new life in Jesus. And having witnessed the birth of two human beings, now I can assuredly tell you that new life is messy. New life involves blood, sweat, tears, stink, pain – but what a rush! What an adventure! I'm praying for you as you start the adventure, and my hope is that at the end of the journey you can yell with great joy – "ABBA DADDY DO!"

Dr. Jacob Youmans
Austin, Texas
October, 2011

Leilani

My First Day of Kindergarten

Fall

20

Build a Bear

And God said, "Let the land produce living creatures according to their kinds: the livestock, the creatures that move along the ground, and the wild animals, each according to its kind." And it was so. God made the wild animals according to their kinds, the livestock according to their kinds, and all the creatures that move along the ground according to their kinds. And God saw that it was good. (Genesis 1:24-25)

Build-A-Bear® gets it. Yes, they are expensive, and so it's probably not a place you can visit frequently. But every once in a while, it's such a treat to watch the joy on the faces of your children as they create their very own stuffed animals. It's all about the experience. Building it is much more fun than just going out and buying it.

After receiving a few complementary Build-A-Bear gift cards, our family headed off to the mall one Saturday afternoon to create new friends. After some indecisiveness, the girls finally picked their animals – Leilani got a dog, and Maile got a cat. (Of course Build-A-Dog/Cat doesn't sound anywhere near as catchy.) The girls gave names to their new pets. They then picked out a heart, kissed the heart, put the heart inside their animal, and then handed the critter over to a Build-A-Bear employee for it to be stuffed.

This employee did a great job of playing along with the whole experience of the animal coming to life. She put some stuffing into the animal and then handed it back to them for a very important "test." Maile and Leilani were then asked to hug their animals and decide whether they wanted more stuffing, less stuffing, or if their creation was "just right."

When it was Leilani's turn, she took her new dog, Sparkles, hugged it lovingly and exclaimed: "It's perfect!" She was so excited!

. . . . .

We read in the first chapter of Genesis that as God was molding, shaping, and decorating His new world, He took a moment at the end of each day to embrace His creation and exclaim, *It is good!* I can only image how excited God was with each new day. The Author of Creation designed and made everything to be "just right!"

When God created people, the human race, Scripture tells us that we were created in His image (Genesis 1:27). We were created to be perfect! Unfortunately, sin came into the world and has consumed not only the human experience but also all of creation.

Maile has two bedtime friends that have been with her basically since birth. They are old and ratty. They are certainly not as fluffy as they once were, and the color they are now was not part of the original design. "Beary" and "Poopsie" have to go through the washing machine occasionally when they don't smell so good. The reunion after a good washing is priceless to watch! These stuffed friends are certainly not attractive anymore – except to Maile. You see, to Maile, they are the most beautiful things in the world. Maile does not see their imperfections – just perfection. In the same way, Jesus, in His unconditional love, sees us not as old, tired, and worn-out, but as the perfect beings He originally created us to be. He longs to pick you up, squeeze you tightly, and proclaim you as "perfect!"

Pray about It

Dear Father,
   You are the creator of all things. Thank You for the blessed and abundant life You have given each one of us. Thank you, too, for loving us so deeply in spite of our flaws and imperfections. I pray that my family and I will always be a reflection of that amazing love, and that we will point others to You. In Jesus' name, Amen.

Talk about It

- God's love for you is amazingly boundless, and it is always available. How can you remind yourself each day of the power and presence of this incredible love?

- Do you ever find yourself defining your self-worth by the measure of your own personal successes and failures? Instead, how can you tie your self-worth to God's promise of unconditional acceptance and love?

Live It Out

Create something together as a family. It can be anything: a picture, a story, a new recipe, or a new game you can play together. Let each person, regardless of age, have a chance to add something to the creation.

Hide and Seek

Where can I go from your Spirit?
  Where can I flee from your presence?
If I go up to the heavens, you are there;
  if I make my bed in the depths, you are there.
If I rise on the wings of the dawn,
  if I settle on the far side of the sea,
even there your hand will guide me,
  your right hand will hold me fast.
If I say, "Surely the darkness will hide me
  and the light become night around me,"
even the darkness will not be dark to you;
  the night will shine like the day,
  for darkness is as light to you. (Psalm 139:7-12)

For a young child, there's nothing quite as exciting as a game of hide-and-seek. There's the fun of scurrying around and searching for a hiding spot, followed by the suspense of whether or not you'll be found. My girls adore playing hide-and-seek. For some reason, they usually designate me as "it" while they scamper off to hide in the house or in the backyard. Of course, it's usually painfully obvious where their hiding places are. There are telltale signs. A shoe or hair bow will be sticking out, or there are visible footprints, or perhaps they have left a mess in their struggle to crawl into a hiding spot.

Of course, part of the fun is actually being found. Sometimes

I find them right away – because they shouldn't win every time, right? And they are always amazed that I found them. "Daddy, how did you find me?" they ask in total disbelief, even when they've hidden in the same spot 14 times in a row!

There are other times when the hiding is not as much fun. Like the time I heard a crash – and then the hurried scrambling of little feet. As I went to investigate what happened, I saw the broken glass on the floor, but no one around. Hmm. I wonder who could have dropped the glass?

The funny thing about running and hiding out of fear is that they still *want* to be found! They may not realize it at first, because guilt and shame consume them. But they *do* want to be found. They want to confess. They want forgiveness. They want someone to care enough about them to seek them out, no matter what they have done wrong, and to say "I love you."

· · · · ·

Childlike faith can be like a game of hide-and-seek. When Adam and Eve first fell into sin, they hid from God's presence (Genesis 3:7-10). But they knew that because He is God, He would therefore know where they were hiding. Even though they did something against God's plan, God still sought them out and found them. It's good to be found! We all have a need to be found, forgiven, and restored in a right relationship with God the Father.

The psalmist in Psalm 139 asks God, "**Where can I flee from your presence?**" It's actually a trick question. You can't. He's everywhere! King David, who wrote this Psalm, did plenty of hiding himself. And he had to learn the hard way how painful "fleeing" can be. But he also knew the unconditional love of a God who is always seeking us. God knows us from the inside out. He knows all our favorite hiding spots. He knows the sins we've committed, and the mess we leave behind, and He still pursues us with a relentless "seeking."

God is seeking *you*. And no matter how clever you are at hiding, He'll find you. He longs to wrap His arms around you and remind you how much you're loved. He wants us to reunite with Him and reminds us that He is always with us wherever we go.

By the way, in the game hide-and-seek, once you've been found you now become the seeker. In the same way, when Jesus finds you and you become His follower, you are then called to seek others – **"to seek and to save the lost"** (Luke 19:10). And never forget about the great rejoicing when the lost is found! (cf. Luke 15:7)

Pray about It

Dear Father,
   Thank You for seeking me out, especially when I feel ashamed and guilty, and don't want to be found! For in those times, when You reach out Your arms to embrace me and comfort me in my embarrassment, I am astounded by Your love and mercy. Teach me to seek You out in the same way You constantly seek me, and help me to show You to others! In the name of Jesus I pray, Amen.

Talk about It

- No matter what we have done, and in our worst moments as well as in our best, God never stops (or even slows down!) in His pursuit of us. How does this truth change the way you approach and interact with God?

- God sets a powerful example of how we are to seek out and love one another. Who in your life desperately needs someone to pursue them and show God's amazing love?

Live It Out

Search for a new place where you can seek out one-on-one time with God. A hike, the beach, a coffee shop? Try a different place each week. Be creative, and go. You're it!

Walking

I have fought the good fight, I have finished the race, I have kept the faith. Now there is in store for me the crown of righteousness, which the Lord, the righteous Judge, will award to me on that day – and not only to me, but also to all who have longed for his appearing. (2 Timothy 4:7-8)

When Maile was first learning how to walk, I loved to watch her. She seemed so focused on figuring out how to balance and position herself, stumbling and stretching more with each passing moment. It's so much fun to watch someone figure out such a vital skill that they will be doing for the rest of their lives.

One Sunday morning, toward the beginning of her walking phase, Maile entered the church gymnasium during the Fellowship Hour. She looked adorable, all dressed up in her "Sunday best." She scanned the crowded room until she spotted Daddy over on the other side of the gym, and fixed her sight on him. The whole basketball court separated us, but she didn't care – she just started toddling toward me. She had just figured out the mechanics of walking and hadn't really advanced to running yet. So to best describe what her movements looked like, you have to picture a one-year-old who walks with one step, and then runs with the next, and then catches herself – and the pattern continues on and on.

After a few steps, she lost one of her shoes. She paid no attention and kept going, hobbling along with one stocking foot and one tiny shoe. After a few more steps, she lost her balance, but didn't fall down. Still, she continued on, her gaze locked on Daddy. She took a few more steps and then the bow in her hair fell out. A large lock of her hair fell down in front of her eyes, but she simply brushed it aside and kept going. Soon the other shoe tumbled off, and with its departure, she hit the ground. But she popped right back up and kept moving. All the way across the gym, her focus remained intent, and she never lost sight of me. She could see the finish line, and her loving father waiting for her with open arms.

After what seemed like days, she finally made it across the gym. A huge grin covered her little face. And never looking back at the long, difficult journey, she fell at last into my arms. She had made it! It wasn't easy, but she had fought the good fight; she had finished the race. She was with Daddy!

· · · · ·

In 2 Timothy 4, St. Paul says the same thing in regard to his life's journey. He has fought the good fight; he has finished the race. It wasn't a perfect fight or race by any stretch of the imagination. He started the race by arresting and killing Christians. He encountered Jesus in the form of a blinding light, and was healed of his blindness three days later. The man who healed his eyesight was told by God that Saul/Paul would learn what it means to suffer for Jesus' name – and did he ever! Prison, public beatings, snake bites (I hate snakes!), shipwrecks, losing friends, and something he describes as a "thorn in his flesh" – all of this was experienced by Paul! I would have quit. In fact, he had plenty of opportunities to quit. But he didn't, because Jesus was his focus, pulling Paul forward and graciously allowing him to finish the race.

Chances are, you won't have to endure prison, public beatings, or a shipwreck. But you will probably experience financial stress, heartache from a loved one who has wronged you, betrayal from a friend, and countless other challenges and disappointments. How can you keep your eyes focused on Jesus? We often think of this as a profound question, but the answers are ancient and simple: Pray. Read the Bible. Surround yourself with people who love you, and who love Jesus. Worship. Serve. It sounds simple, I suppose, but it works!

Life is a journey. It has ups and downs. There are going to be times when our shoes fall off, we lose our balance and fall down. But great is the reward for those who believe in Christ Jesus, and focus their eyes upon Him! Let's keep progressing in this journey of life, step by step. Feel free to walk, run, or crawl – but just keep moving by faith!

Pray about It

Dear Father,

So often during difficult times, I struggle to remain focused and Christ-centered. But in Your compassion, You still reach out Your loving arms to me and fully accept me when I return to You. Without Your love and forgiveness, my failures would overwhelm me. Gracious God, please give me the strength and motivation to keep pressing on, all for Your glory. In Jesus' name, Amen.

Talk about It

- Paul talks of running and finishing the race, but more importantly he reminds us that he *keeps* the faith as he does it (cf. 2 Timothy 4). All too often, we focus too intently on reaching the finish line, but neglect important things along the way. In the journey of life, what important aspects of your faith do you sometimes let slide? How can you keep your focus on Christ?

- Life is filled with ups and downs. As we travel through the mountaintops and valleys, our faith will be tested and challenged. Which do you believe teaches us more about ourselves and our faith – the "ups" or the "downs?"

Live It Out

Sign up for a local charity 5K or walkathon that you and your family can participate in together. Gather pledges to sponsor your group for every mile of the course. Afterwards, discuss the event. What challenges and distractions did you encounter as you journeyed for the finish line? What helped you keep your focus?

Friends

I no longer call you servants, because a servant does not know his master's business. Instead, I have called you friends, for everything that I learned from my Father I have made known to you. (John 15:15)

I'll never forget the first day of first grade for my firstborn, Maile. During the summer months, we had moved from California to Texas, and August had already been a month filled with many new experiences. Maile was so eager for school to begin, and she had been excitedly counting down the days on the kitchen calendar. Now the big day had finally arrived.

I have always loved walking my daughters to school in the morning. It's our time to talk, sing, or tell stories. Every morning is a bit different, but we always enjoy our special time together as we head into a new day filled with adventures and possibilities.

As we walked down the street that first morning on our way to her new school, Maile was skipping along happily beside me. She was wearing her new "first day of school" clothes, her new backpack (which was very pink and girlie), and toted a special snack in her sister's lunch box (also very pink and girlie) which she had borrowed that morning because she couldn't find her own at the last minute.

But after a few blocks, I started to notice that Maile's happy, bouncing steps weren't so happy and bouncing anymore. Her pace had slowed, and her smile had faded. I could feel her apprehension grow with every step she took toward the school building. This didn't surprise me, and in fact I had been expecting it. Maile's new school here in Texas was three times the size of her old one in California. She didn't know a soul yet. I knew that walking into a loud, bustling elementary school filled with 1,500 kids who were all completely new to her would be a bit intimidating, even for my social butterfly, Maile.

I was wondering how to bring up the topic to her when Maile turned to me with a worried expression and blurted out, "Daddy, what if I don't make any friends here?"

"Oh sweetie, don't worry," I reassured her. "You're going to make lots of friends!"

"But I miss my friends in California," she continued. "I miss my school there, and all my teachers. I miss *everything* back there."

I squeezed her hand in mine. "Me too, honey. It's hard to leave friends behind. But I really believe you are going to make lots of new friends at this new school. Jesus knows that you need friends here. He knows we all need good friends in our lives. And He will always give us the things we need. Let's pray to Him right now and ask Him to bless you with new friends today." And so we prayed aloud together as we walked those last few blocks to school, putting our worries into His hands.

· · · · ·

Friends – we all need them! Friends are the ones who are with us through the good times and the bad. They are the people who know all about us – who we are, and what we are all about – and amazingly enough, they still like us anyway! Friends are a powerful way through which God continues to bless us all through our lives here on earth. Friends are vital to our emotional well-being as well as our spiritual growth. And when you've uprooted your whole family and moved halfway across the country to a brand-new community, you realize more than ever just how important friends really are!

Jesus does something wonderful for us in John 15:15. He calls us *friends*. He expresses His desire to be in an intimate relationship with us, and He tells us that we are no longer to be called servants – who are only valued based on the work they do – but friends. If you do a little study of the other world religions, you will discover that none of them have anything close to this idea of a greater being, or creator, calling human beings "friends." As we sing in the comforting, familiar hymn:

> ***What a friend we have in Jesus,***
> ***All our sins and griefs to bear!***
> ***What a privilege to carry***
> ***Everything to God in prayer!***
> (Joseph M. Scriven, 1855)

Jesus is a true friend who is always with us, no matter what we do, or where we go. Jesus also understands our need for friendships, and He provides and blesses us with meaningful people in our lives. When Maile returned home from that first day of first grade, she excitedly announced that she had made four new friends! I knew that was just the beginning. What a friend we have in Jesus!

Pray about It

Dear Jesus,

I am so honored that You would call me Your friend! You know everything about me, all of my flaws, imperfections, and sins, and yet You still want to be with me so much that You sacrificed Your own life to save mine. Thank You for such an incredible gift! Stir in me the desire to spend time with You each day in prayer and in the Word, for Your friendship is the greatest of all. In Your name I pray, Amen.

Talk about It

- As well as being described as our King, our Shepherd, our Savior, and our Lord, Scripture also describes Jesus as our friend (John 15:15). What new dimension(s) does this add to your view of God and the way in which you interact with Him?

- How much time do you spend in fellowship with your friend Jesus, compared to your earthly friends? Is this a good balance?

Live It Out

Encourage each family member to try to make a new friend this week in school, at work, or on the playground. Look for someone who needs befriending. Ask God to use you as a blessing in this person's life.

The Truth

Truthful lips endure forever, but a lying tongue lasts only a moment. (Proverbs 12:19)

"Leilani has a rock stuck up her nose and we can't get it out. Could you come down here?" pleaded the voice on the phone.

I had to ask her to repeat the statement a few times before I understood what had happened. *She has a rock stuck up her nose?* How does that even happen?

I ran over to the preschool and found my little girl sitting on a bench on the playground. A crowd had gathered around her. The adults were huddled together, trying to figure out what to do. Leilani's classmates were sitting beside her, keeping her company, curious to see how the rock was going to be extracted from her nose. Leilani was sitting there calmly and courageously in the midst of all the fuss and concern. But as soon as she saw me walking over to her, she let the tears flow. So of course I ran to her and hugged her, assuring her that everything was going to be okay – even though I didn't have any idea how I would ever get this thing out of her nose.

One of the preschool teachers handed me a little pair of tweezers, and as I tipped Leilani's head back a bit, I gently tried to coax the rock out. I quickly realized that this wasn't going to be easy. The rock was just the perfect size and shape to get wedged in there tightly. I couldn't get a grip on it with the tweezers even after numerous attempts. I didn't want to panic Leilani, but I started to doubt whether we'd be able to get it out without a trip to the emergency room.

Next, I tried having her blow her nose hard, hoping to dislodge it somehow. Nothing. Finally, I knew it was time to get serious. This rock was not going to win – it was coming out! I laid her down, tilted her head back, and inserted the tweezers one last time. And suddenly, I was able to get a hold of it. In an instant, the rock was finally out! There was great rejoicing – and no blood!

After the celebration died down, I walked her back to her classroom, just the two of us – hand in hand, sharing the moment. At that point, I just had to ask the big question that was on everyone's mind.

"Leilani, how'd that rock get in your nose?"

"I don't know!" she exclaimed, still clearly traumatized by the whole incident.

I didn't want to upset her further; it had been a stressful morning. So I dropped her off in her classroom, kissed her good-bye, and went back to work.

That evening at home, Leilani showed the rock to her mom and sister, recounting the story of Daddy's heroic rock retrieval skills. We put the rock into a little film canister to keep it as a souvenir of sorts. I thought it was time to ask her the big question again.

"Leilani, are you sure you don't know how that rock got in your nose?"

"Daddy, it just bounced up there when we were in the sand-box," she replied.

Hmm. I've been in my fair share of sandboxes over the years, but I don't recall ever seeing any bouncing stones. But again, I didn't want to push her. I knew she would tell me when she was ready.

A few days later, Leilani came to me. "Daddy, remember that rock that was in my nose?"

Remember? Yep, that's one I won't soon forget! "Of course I do, honey. What about it?"

"Well, it was in my shoe after playing in the sandbox, and I wanted to know if it smelled like my shoe. So I put it in my nose to smell it, and then it got stuck there."

Ah, now it all made sense! "Wow! Honey, why didn't you tell me the truth in the first place?"

"I didn't want you to be mad at me," she admitted.

"Leilani, we always need to tell the truth. And yes, sometimes I might get mad. But if I do, it's only because I love you, and the most important job I have is to keep you safe. Do you understand?"

Leilani threw her arms around me, relieved to have finally told me the truth. I was relieved too, that she shared the real story with me. I had imagined various scenarios as to how that rock had found its way up her nose, although I have to admit that none of them came anywhere close to what really happened!

. . . . .

What a relief to know the truth! In our dealings with other people, the truth can sometimes be elusive. What a contrast this is to our relationship with God where we know from Scripture that He can be nothing other than truthful with us! In the books written by St. John, there are many references to the connection between Jesus and Truth. Probably one of the most familiar is John 14:6, where Jesus says: **"I am the way and the truth and the life. No one comes to the Father except through me."** Man-made religions are based on ideas that can seem logical to us – for example, "getting right with God" by doing good works – but the Truth is something so gloriously unexpected that we never could have conceived of it if left to our own imaginations.

Yes, what a relief it is to know the Truth! The freedom it brings is well-expressed in John 8:31-32, where Jesus says: **"If you hold to my teaching, you are really my disciples. Then you will know the truth, and the truth will set you free."** The freedom Jesus speaks about is much more complex than life in prison or as a civilian in a dictatorship, but it is also very tangible. It's freedom from guilt. It's freedom to hold one's head high because there is no shame. It's freedom from the vicious circle of lies that are constantly created to cover up past lies. It's freedom to pursue one's God-given dreams with no regrets. It's forgiveness. It's love. It's knowing that there's nothing so big in your past or in your future that Jesus can't handle. Yes, in Jesus there is freedom from all of our burdens! May God grant you the joy that comes from experiencing true freedom, and may He guide your steps as you continue to walk in the Truth (cf. 3 John 1:3-4).

Pray about It

Dear Jesus,

Your love for the world is truthful and honest. I pray that each day I will follow Your example to engage truthfully in my relationships with You, my family, and others. I am privileged to know that You *are* the Way, the Truth, and the Life – and it is an amazing blessing to be able to share that truth with others! In Your name I pray, Amen.

Talk about It

• We sometimes make excuses as to why it is okay to lie in certain situations. We call those instances "white lies." But is lying ever justifiable? Do you think God regards some lies as excusable?

• What truths about ourselves are we withholding from God? Are we always honest with Him? What do we have to confess that we've been hiding from Him?

Live It Out

During your next gathering with family or friends, play the game "Two Truths and a Lie." The rules of this game are simple: each person comes up with two truths and one lie about themselves and then shares them with the group. The group's goal is to discern which statements are true and which is false. Talk about the game as you play it. Is it hard to distinguish what is true? What makes you believe certain things are true and not others?

42

Dress-Up

Therefore put on the full armor of God, so that when the day of evil comes, you may be able to stand your ground, and after you have done everything, to stand. Stand firm then, with the belt of truth buckled around your waist, with the breastplate of righteousness in place, and with your feet fitted with the readiness that comes from the gospel of peace. In addition to all this, take up the shield of faith, with which you can extinguish all the flaming arrows of the evil one. Take the helmet of salvation and the sword of the Spirit, which is the word of God. (Ephesians 6:13-17)

Maile and Leilani love to play dress-up. In fact, they own more fantasy clothes than I have articles of clothing in my entire closet. Their dress-up collection is huge. They have miniature versions of all the Disney princess dresses. They own several dresses from the Barbie® movies. They have some outfits modeled after Hannah Montana. If the Disney studios ever find themselves running short in the wardrobe department, they can come over to our house and find anything they might need! Make no mistake – every single one of these garments is very important to my girls. Once, I made the mistake of suggesting that they might not really *need* all fifty-three princess dresses. Oops! That didn't go over very well. How silly of me! They insist that they can perform and play properly only when they are wearing just the right dress-up clothes. I think they might even enjoy the dressing-up aspect of Halloween as much as (if not more than) collecting all the candy!

The girls are constantly fighting over who gets to be the princess and who gets stuck playing the part of the queen (I once thought that being the queen was a good thing!) or even worse – who has to be the prince! Apparently the princess is the top role, and they both want it. They insist that there cannot be two princesses – although I don't understand why not. At times I've tried to explain to them that in a constitutional monarchy, the princess really has nothing to do, but they just ignore me and keep playing.

· · · · ·

What is it about dress-up that's so much fun? Think about how Halloween seems to bring out the creative side in even the most boring and stodgy people we know. We all enjoy a chance to try on a different character for a while, and to become something we normally aren't. What we wear can influence how we feel about ourselves, as well as how others perceive us. Those who wear a uniform as part of their profession often say that the clothing they wear for the job makes them feel more competent and empowered for service. It gives them an air of confidence and strength that they wouldn't normally have if they were in street clothes. Their words and actions are often greatly influenced by it as well.

St. Paul encourages all followers of Jesus to play a little dress-up in Ephesians 6:10-17. This well-known section of Scripture describes putting on the "full armor of God." Paul was sitting in jail when he wrote this letter to the church in Ephesus. As he observed the Roman guards day in and day out, he realized the power of a good game of dress-up. Listen to the garments he lays out for us to wear: the belt of truth, the breastplate of righteousness, the shoes of the readiness of the gospel, the shield of faith, the helmet of salvation, and finally the sword of the Spirit. That's quite an impressive outfit!

Maybe it's time you played a little dress-up. Start by putting on each of these important pieces of armor.

What will that belt of truth look like around your waist as you go to work, or spend time with your family? How will following Him who is the Truth (John 14:6) influence your own words and decisions?

What about that breastplate of righteousness? It will certainly guard your heart as well as make for interesting "chest bump" celebrations. Doing the right thing when it's the hard thing is something we try so hard to teach our children; as we wear this breastplate, we get to model it for them.

What if your feet were fitted with the readiness that comes from the gospel of peace? I know that's a mouthful – but it's also a foot-full! We are called to be always ready. The battle is all around us, and at any moment we can be engaged in it. And in the heat of the battle we are reminded that God is a God of peace.

What about the shield of faith? How would that look on your arm? Remember that while a shield is best known for being a defensive weapon, it's also used to attack. Faith extinguishes the flames of the Devil, but it also transforms you into a battering ram to get you through the enemy line.

How about the helmet of salvation? That will certainly guard your mind – knowing that no matter what happens on this earth, heaven is your home.

And finally, you are armed with the sword of the Spirit, which is the word of God. Be careful – this sword is sharp! We're told it's double-edged in Hebrews 4:12. This sword cuts straight to the heart, as these are the words of the God of the Universe. This sword is the "power" that Jesus Himself promised us in Acts 1:8.

This outfit transforms you. It makes you fearless! When in this armor, whom would you fear? 1 John 4:4 reminds us that greater is the One who lives inside of us than the one who lives in the world. Now that's dress-up!

Pray about It

Dear Father,

Thank You for equipping me with the perfect wardrobe to be protected from evil. Your armor is complete, and can withstand anything that Satan throws my way. Remind me to consciously and deliberately put on these pieces of armor each day, knowing You are indeed with me. In the name of Your Son Jesus Christ I pray, Amen.

Talk about It

- Which piece of spiritual armor has been the easiest and most comfortable for you to wear throughout your daily life? Which piece has been the heaviest and most difficult for you to strap on and wear? Are there any vulnerable spots in your armor that need reinforcing?

- There is an old saying that goes: "The best defense is a good offense." How can we use these pieces of armor not only to defend ourselves from Satan's attacks, but also to prevent them from striking us at all?

Live It Out

Most of us have at least one closet in our home that is stuffed with items of clothing that are seldom worn. Why not share your abundance with those who have much less? Choose a day to completely weed through this closet, evaluating each piece of clothing carefully and keeping only your absolute favorites. Put the rest of the clothing in a box and drop it off at a local women's crisis shelter or other agency that will distribute the clothing to those in need.

48

When You Get It, You Go

Then Jesus came to them and said, "All authority in heaven and on earth has been given to me. Therefore go and make disciples of all nations, baptizing them in the name of the Father and of the Son and of the Holy Spirit, and teaching them to obey everything I have commanded you. And surely I am with you always, to the very end of the age." (Matthew 28:18-20)

Oh, the joys of Halloween! My daughters have loved it from their very first exposure to it. They absolutely love candy, and therefore any holiday that involves collecting massive quantities of free candy is an occasion they don't want to miss!

When Maile was only eighteen months old, she experienced trick-or-treating for the first time. She dressed up as a fuzzy duck. I don't remember how she ended up as a duck, but I have to admit, she was the cutest duck I had ever seen!

Maile was small for her age. She was actually in the zero percentile for a while, which supposedly means that 100% of kids her age were bigger than her. I'm still not sure how that's possible. I check in at 6' 2" and 220 pounds, and her pediatrician always told us that she's all Daddy... except for her size! Maile was still mastering her walking skills as well at this point. She wobbled a bit as she moved, and much preferred being carried by Daddy.

Christy was eight months pregnant with our second daughter, Leilani, and not surprisingly didn't want to go trick-or-treating that night. So I knew it was up to me to teach my daughter all the ins and outs of this wonderful ritual. I was so excited about it. I was looking forward to it even more than she was!

I helped Maile get dressed up in her duck costume. Grasping the handle of her pumpkin bucket in her tiny hand, she quacked a few times and headed out the door. We walked next door to our neighbor's house. Maile rang the doorbell and waited patiently for someone to answer. I was so proud of her. This was the very first house of her very first Halloween!

Now, I should explain that at this point in her life, Maile couldn't really talk yet. So when the door finally opened, she simply held out her bucket. The woman who answered that door literally melted at the sight of this adorable little duck with her candy bucket! And she threw handfuls of candy into Maile's bucket.

Maile's eyes grew wider than I had ever seen them in her eighteen months of life. She got it! She quickly figured out how Halloween worked, after only one house! At the next house, she rang the door bell again. But this time when someone opened the door, Maile kicked up her duck performance a few notches. She flapped her arms like they were wings and quacked as she set her bucket down in front of the opened door. Again, our neighbor found her irresistibly cute, and more handfuls of candy were Maile's reward. So of course, after thanking them politely, she was off to the next house as quickly as her little legs could carry her!

Originally I had planned to visit only about half a block of our neighborhood that night, just to give her a taste of the potential that Halloween presented. I didn't want to wear her out on her very first year. However, four blocks later, Maile was still going! She could no longer lift her pumpkin bucket due to the quantity of candy. And even at the young age of eighteen months, she already knew that she couldn't give her candy to Daddy to hold because there's a very good chance he'd eat it. Smart girl!

As I watched her hurry down the sidewalk that evening, it hit me. When you get it, you go. Maile got it, and she couldn't help but run from house to house in her excitement. Candy was her reward, and she wasn't going to stop until she got as much as possible. When you get it, you go!

. . . . .

That's the Great Commission in a nutshell. We're called in Matthew chapter 28 to "**GO.**" The Scriptures are full of people who got it and then had to go. Moses was raised as a prince of Egypt in the lap of luxury, and then ran away in fear for his own life. But when the command came through a burning bush – he had to go! David was a shepherd boy who took care of his father's sheep, but when a giant threatened God's people – he had to go! Saul was a Pharisee of Pharisees, so zealous for Yahweh that he was eliminating the world of the "cult" of Jesus of Nazareth. But when he encountered the same Jesus on the road to Damascus – he had to go!

When we "get" what Jesus has done for us, when we understand that it was love that held Him to the cross, and love that enabled Him to rise from the dead, we gotta go! We can't wait to go tell the whole world what Jesus has done, because it changes everything! We want to share our faith with everyone we meet. Invite a neighbor to church. Offer to pray with a friend in need. Help someone who thinks they're helpless.

Great is the reward for the followers of Jesus, not only in the promise of eternal life in heaven but also here in this earthly life! When you get it, you go!

Pray about It

Dear Father,
    May the Holy Spirit work powerfully in my heart to excite and motivate me to action. Send me out into the world to share the good news that Your Son, Jesus Christ died for our sins! Please give me the courage I need, and grant that fear and uncertainty won't stand in the way of just "going!" In Jesus' name I pray, Amen.

Talk about It

- Scripture tells us that when Saul opened his eyes after being blinded on the road to Damascus, he realized what was holding him back, and then he could see again (cf. Acts 9:17). Where are some of the blind spots in your faith life?

- The best way to encourage our children to go forth and enthusiastically share their faith with the world is to set the example for them to follow. How can you help equip others to "go?"

Live It Out

As a family, make a list of some practical ways you can share your faith – through words and actions – with others in your community. Choose one of these ideas and decide to follow through on it together this week.

The Offering

Let them give thanks to the LORD for his unfailing love
and his wonderful deeds for mankind.
Let them sacrifice thank offerings
and tell of his works with songs of joy. (Psalm 107:21-22)

One of the things we have always tried to teach our two girls is the importance of giving back to God. We've explained that God has given us such an abundance of blessings, and it's our privilege to share them in turn with others. They've watched me collect the offering during many church services over the years, and they've always been encouraged to set aside a portion of their allowance to give back to God. From a young age, putting their money into the offering plate on Sunday has been a source of great joy for them each week.

So I probably shouldn't have been too surprised to hear that Maile had a tearful meltdown one morning at preschool – all because she had forgotten to bring her offering envelope for chapel!

At first, her teachers couldn't figure out what was wrong. The other kids were lined up at the classroom door, preparing to walk down to the church for Wednesday morning chapel service, but Maile sat at her desk, sobbing uncontrollably. The teachers thought perhaps she felt sick, or that someone had hurt her feelings. But finally Maile was able to explain through her tears that she had forgotten her offering envelope on the kitchen table at home – and now she had nothing to give to God.

The teachers didn't quite know how to react. They were very used to dealing with kids in tears, but not for a reason like this! Maile was inconsolable. They tried to get a hold of me in my office at church, but I was in a meeting across town. Then they explained the situation to the church secretary, and she kindly gave Maile a few coins for her offering. Maile gratefully wiped away the tears and then joined the rest of her class in chapel. Whew – disaster averted! Maile was so happy that she was still able to put her offering in the basket that morning. Now, even years later, Maile's preschool teachers still talk about that incident. They still haven't seen anything quite like it!

· · · · ·

In Psalm 107:22, the Psalmist says, **"Let them sacrifice thank offerings and tell of his works with songs of joy."** Okay, so he doesn't quite say, "If you forget your offering, cry uncontrollably." But I think there's still a good point there. It is truly a joy and a privilege for us to give something back to our God who has given us so much! Too often, we grumble when we put our money in the offering plate. Perhaps somewhere in the back of our heads, as we write out that check, our brain is flipping through a list of all the other things we could buy with that money. Or maybe we question the stewardship of our congregation, and whether our gifts will be used in the way we'd prefer to see them used. When these things happen, we start looking at giving as a burden – an obligation – something we *have* to do. But that's completely missing the spirit of an "offering." The offering is a love letter from our hearts, a thankful response to God's grace and goodness. God doesn't need our money, but we need to give!

When, for whatever reason, we choose not to share our blessings, we are missing out on the special joy of giving that God has designed for us. Reflect on the passage above from Psalm 107, and the next time the offering plate passes by, or when a homeless person asks for a dollar, or when a letter comes from a charitable organization, remember that it's a joy to give back to the One who has given us everything we have!

Pray about It

Dear Father,
  May it always be a joy for me to give back to You! Remind me that my offerings are used to glorify You in so many ways. Thank you for being so generous to me, and for all of the amazing blessings You have given to me. I pray that You will now use me, in turn, to be a blessing to Your church and to others, all for Your glory. In Jesus' name I pray, Amen.

Talk about It

- Sometimes we let our own selfishness and pride get in the way of many things in our lives, including our offerings. Have you been holding back from God in your personal life? Financially? In time with the Word? In worship?

- What are some ways that you can more actively involve your entire family in the giving process?

Live It Out

Think of a creative way to bless one of God's children with an offering. Perhaps you can buy a homeless person on the street a hearty lunch. Or better yet, *ask* them what they could really use, and get it for them. Remind them that they are loved by God.

Pray Like a Child

Rejoice always, pray continually, give thanks in all cir-cumstances; for this is God's will for you in Christ Jesus.
(1 Thessalonians 5:16-18)

I love listening to my children pray. It's beautiful. It's simple. It's straight from their little hearts. Christy and I have inten-tionally not taught them any memorized or recited prayers. It's not that there's anything wrong with those types of prayers, but we want our kids to talk to God just as they would talk to us – in a personal, spontaneous, intimate way. We want our girls to feel comfortable spilling their hearts, minds, and souls to their heavenly Father, without feeling that it's necessary to follow a particular formula or recitation.

But what's funny is that every single night, both of our girls choose to start their prayers with the same specific phrase: *"Dear Jesus, thank You for this wonderful day!"*

Now, don't get me wrong. That's a great way to start your prayers! But is *every* single day really a "wonderful day?"

Some days really *are* wonderful. Sometimes we spend the entire day at Disneyland, followed by dinner at Chuck E. Cheese's, and then we top it all off with a huge ice cream sundae. Now, those are *truly* wonderful days!

But some days are not so wonderful. Sometimes the girls spend most of the day in their rooms by themselves – grounded for fighting, not listening, lying, arguing, or misbehaving.

Sometimes a day is difficult and painful, such as when a relative or friend dies, or when the girls both wake up sick, throwing up from the stomach flu. Even when our own sin isn't to blame for our bad days, we still live in a sinful world – and there will always be sickness, death, setbacks, and disappointments. Unfortunately, not-so-wonderful days do occur.

And yet, whether it's a Disneyland day, a "grounded" day, or a stomach flu day, the girls still offer up the same prayer: *"Dear Jesus, thank You for this wonderful day!"*

· · · · ·

In 1 Thessalonians 5, we're told to "**rejoice always**" (verse 16) and to "**give thanks in all circumstances**" (verse 18). Now, we all know that it's very easy to rejoice and give thanks at Disneyland, but it's much more difficult on the days when we are hurting, disappointed, sick, or grieving. What we need to appreciate is that true joy and thanksgiving do not come out of external circumstances. Gratitude comes from a realization of the inner workings of Jesus. No matter what happens, Jesus still loves us. When we can see Jesus at work in ALL circumstances – in the happy times and in the difficult times – then we can honestly pray: "Dear Jesus, thank You for this wonderful day!"

Pray about It

Dear Jesus,

Thank You for this wonderful day! Your grace is eternal and Your love is abundant in every single day. Forgive me when I can't always see that goodness, especially when times are hard and my heart is hurting, and I seem ungrateful for what You've provided. Help me to give thanks in *all* circumstances. Thank You for making even the most difficult days a blessing because You love me! I pray this in Your name, Amen.

Talk about It

- Prayer is such a pure and simple act. Yet, how often do we think of it as something that should take place at certain times or in certain places, or something that we need to recite in a certain way. What are some of the things that are holding you back from praying more spontaneously?

- In Psalm 51, David cries out for a pure heart. What does it mean to pray with your heart? Do you ever pray with your mind rather than with your heart?

Live It Out

During the next week, try starting all of your prayers by thanking God for the wonderful day He has give you. Focus on the blessings He has given you even in the midst of the most difficult circumstances you face this week.

Thank You!

Praise the Lord. Give thanks to the Lord, for he is good; his love endures forever. (Psalm 106:1)

Teaching our kids to be polite and respectful is very important to us. We want them to learn to be considerate of other people, their possessions, and their needs. We desire compassion and kindness. From a young age, our girls have been taught how to use the "magic" words of please and thank you – and then use them for the rest of their lives. I am constantly prompting them with, "Now what do you say?" to encourage them to insert "please" or "thank you" at the appropriate time. Sometimes I wish they expressed a little more sincerity and genuine appreciation in the "thank you" part. But they are on the right track.

Recently, I questioned Leilani about the actual meaning of these "magic" words. Leilani had an interesting response. "'Please' is when you want something," she explained, "and 'thank you' means you got it."

. . . . .

It's true, isn't it? Most of us tend to say "thank you" only after we get something we want. But how often do we initiate a "thank you" for something we haven't asked for? How often do we thank someone just for being wonderful, loving, and kind? How often do we say "thank You" to God for all He has done for us?

Sometimes we simply forget. Sure, it's easy for us to remember to thank God when He has answered our urgent prayers – when He heals us from sickness, keeps us safe in a dangerous situation, or blesses us with a long-awaited child. But in other times, we tend to forget to lift our hearts to God and simply say, "Thank You for all that You are – almighty, all-knowing, merciful. Thank You for creating this beautiful world around us. Thank You for loving us so much that You sent Jesus to be the atoning sacrifice for our sins. Thank You for preparing a place for us with You in heaven."

We are told throughout the Bible to give thanks to the Lord. The wording, **"Give thanks to the Lord, for He is good; His love endures forever"** is repeated six times in Scripture, and there are many more close variations. Thankfulness is extremely important to God. Why does He want our gratitude? Simply put, because He deserves it. He wants us to be ever mindful of the fact that He is the source of all goodness. God wants our appreciation to be driven by more than just our selfish gain when we get something we've asked for. We are to give thanks to God because He is good, righteous, and faithful. His love remains with us forever. We give thanks to God for sending us Jesus, and for His forgiveness and salvation. Our thanksgiving is also a powerful witness to others, because as we give credit to Him for all He has done in our lives, we are telling the world that He is the One True God.

After a recent sleepover, Leilani came home and came right up to me and whispered in my ear, "Daddy, Emma's Daddy said that I was the most polite little girl he's ever met!"

"Wow!" I said. "That's awesome! Why do you think he said that?"

"Because every time he gave me anything – even if I didn't want it – I said, 'Thank you'!"

That made me pretty proud… and thankful!

Give thanks in all circumstances (1 Thessalonians 5:18)! This isn't always easy, but it is God's will for our lives. May God grant you the peace that comes from giving praise and thanks to Him each and every day – even the ones that are challenging for us. Remember – He is faithful and will not forsake us (cf. Hebrews 13:5-6). Yet another thing to be thankful for!

Pray about It

Dear Father,

Thank You for everything You do in my life, and for everything You provide for my family. Thank You especially for all the numerous blessings that I take for granted, and the ones that I don't readily see. Help me to grow in my thankfulness toward You and others. In Jesus' name, Amen.

Talk about It

- If someone were to follow you around and observe your words and actions for an entire week, do you think they would say that you have a "thankful" lifestyle?

- How would your life change if you actively expressed thanks for God's goodness, especially for the gifts you didn't ask for?

Live It Out

When you sit down to dinner tonight, take a few minutes to go around the table and have each person share something they are thankful for. Try doing this each night for a week, and see how many different reasons you can think of. When you are finished with you meal, read Psalm 106:1 together as your prayer of thankfulness to God.

Winter

70

Important Work

The apostles gathered around Jesus and reported to him all they had done and taught. Then, because so many people were coming and going that they did not even have a chance to eat, he said to them, "Come with me by yourselves to a quiet place and get some rest." (Mark 6:30-31)

One morning while Maile was in school, my wife had a doctor's appointment, so she dropped Leilani off to spend a few hours with Daddy while he worked in his office. Unfortunately, it was one of those busy, catch-up-on-important-work days, so I knew I wouldn't have time to interact with her very much. Instead, I just put on one of her favorite DVDs to occupy her attention, and gave her some paper and markers to draw with. She was delighted by the idea of having her own "important work" to do alongside Daddy, and immediately started drawing.

Leilani was very quiet and didn't disturb me at all as I worked for almost an hour. As preoccupied as I was with working through my own stack of paperwork and answering overdue e-mails, I had almost forgotten that she was even there until she tapped me on the arm.

"Daddy?"

"Just a minute, honey, I need to finish this," I replied without looking up.

"Daddy, I made this picture for you!" She held out her colorful drawing for me to admire.

"Thanks, honey," I said, without even looking at it. I continued to type away on the keyboard.

"Daddy?"

"Just a minute."

"I love coming to work with you!" Leilani exclaimed.

I stopped typing and finally looked up from my "important" work to behold what was *truly* the most important work of my life. There she was, beaming ear to ear – her little heart overflowing with unconditional love for me. Her picture was beautiful. She had drawn a picture of the two of us – purple Leilani and green Daddy – sitting in my office, working together, with huge smiles on our large heads. I absolutely loved it! We proudly hung it on my office door. I turned off my computer, pushed aside my stack of papers, and asked the rhetorical question: "Leilani, do you want to go to McDonald's for lunch?" And off we went to the Golden Arches for a little quality daddy-daughter time.

· · · · ·

Do you ever get so busy with seemingly important work that you push aside the *truly* important work that Jesus wants us to do? It's so easy for us to become distracted and pulled away from what is really meaningful. It's been said that if the devil can't make you bad, he'll make you busy. Too busy for your family. Too busy to go to church. Too busy to pray. Too busy to listen to God's Word and His plan for your life. The world we live in encourages and rewards us to work constantly and to live in a perpetual state of busyness, so we don't even realize we are missing out on the most important and precious things of all. Satan is pretty clever – what an ingenious plan!

Time is our most precious commodity. Even with all of the amazing technology that has been invented to give us more time, we still don't seem to have enough of it. We don't even have time to rest!

Jesus' advice on how to find rest is really pretty simple. He says to the disciples in Mark 6:31: "**Come with me by yourselves to a quiet place and get some rest.**" Similarly, in Matthew 11:28 Jesus says: "**Come to me, all you who are weary and burdened, and I will give you rest.**"

Resting in Him will renew us and give us what we need to carry on. Resting in Him will strengthen our relationship with Him and help us to prioritize what's really important in life. This week – maybe today, maybe even right this moment! – go with Jesus... by yourself... to a quiet place. Turn off the computer and the cell phone, and push aside all the urgency and obligations. Jesus wants us to seek Him in a place with no distractions and interruptions. He wants your full attention and your whole heart. He is the only one who can give you true rest – a rest that surpasses all human understanding, knowledge, creativity, technology, imagination, and ingenuity.

I'm sure your important work will still be there when you get back.

Pray about It

Dear Jesus,

Help me prioritize my life so that I always make plenty of time for You and my family. I pray that all earthly distractions may be pushed aside so my heart will be constantly focused and re-centered around You. Open my eyes with Your wisdom so that I may see what is truly important. In Your name I pray, Amen.

Talk about It

- Which items on your daily schedule threaten to overshadow the things in your life that are truly the most important?

- How much time is devoted each day to strengthening your relationship with Jesus, and to resting in His presence? Is this something you should make a higher priority?

Live It Out

The next time you feel overwhelmed by your endless to-do list of chores, responsibilities, and appointments, try this exercise. Make a conscious decision to put those things aside for a half hour, and go sit down and play a game with your child. The act of putting aside the seemingly urgent for the truly important is a good reminder of your highest priorities – God and family.

Patience

Therefore, as God's chosen people, holy and dearly loved, clothe yourselves with compassion, kindness, humility, gentleness and patience. (Colossians 3:12)

"Daddy!" Leilani screamed from down the hall.

"What?" I screamed right back.

"I need you to get it for me right now!" she replied even louder.

"Honey, you need to be patient," I replied with fatherly wisdom.

"I WILL be patient – if you give it to me right now!" Leilani yelled back.

· · · · ·

Well, okay, maybe she doesn't really understand patience yet. But do any of us? I certainly don't! In the interchange above, I was just as impatient as she was. Patience is just one of those words that's easy to understand but hard to put into practice. And I need to admit that I can't say or hear the word without hearing Axel Rose's voice singing it in my head. Patience wouldn't be so bad... if I could get some right now!

At times, I treat my heavenly Father exactly the same way. "God, I'm being very patient here waiting for You. So will You just give it to me already?!" You've probably heard it said that patience is a virtue – which is something that most parents can appreciate, having experienced times when our own patience has been severely stretched to the limits by our children. Patience is included in the fruit of the Spirit (Galatians 5:22; some translations: "forbearance" or "longsuffering"). But being patient is hard, and it can be downright painful.

King Solomon tells us in Proverbs 19:11, "**A man's wisdom gives him patience.**" (NIV, 1984) But even a wise man could use more patience. Read some of the stories from King Solomon's life. He is widely considered the wisest man who ever lived. In 1 Kings 4:31, it says that "**He (Solomon) was wiser than anyone else.**" But he certainly wasn't the most patient person! He was actually rather impulsive and allowed himself to get caught up in the pleasures of this life. He had thousands of wives and concubines. He experimented in the worship of other gods. He allowed greed to consume him and he overtaxed his people. Despite his wisdom, he ended up damaging the country he loved.

Our human nature doesn't want to wait. It wants instant gratification. Cars, microwaves, cell phones, and countless other inventions were all invented so we could avoid being patient. Patience is difficult!

I've always found my patience to be most tested in my prayer life. When I pray for something, I always want it right now. I don't mind being told "no." I understand "no," but what really is frustrating to me is – "wait." Sometimes God says, "You need to do some growing first." Sometimes God says,

"You need to slow down." These are the hard answers to prayers for me.

Now, Jesus is the perfect example of patience. He was patient with His disciples when they just didn't get it. And He is equally patient with us when we are plagued by doubts and fears. When I get frustrated with the world, I wish that Jesus would just hurry up and come back already. But He's patient. Think of it this way: Jesus' patience might just be our greatest opportunity; we still have time to share His love with a world that needs to hear about His love (cf. 2 Peter 3:9). Lord, thank you for your patience with us, and give us the endurance to treat others with the same loving patience!

Pray about It

Dear Jesus,
   Please forgive me for the impatience in my life. Greed and neediness can sometimes overwhelm my thoughts and prayers. Help me to have complete faith in Your timing and in all the plans that You have in store for me. Allow me to knowingly accept that Your plans are worth the wait! I pray all this in Your holy name, Amen.

Talk about It

- Reflect on a few of the situations in your daily life that often challenge your patience. Can you think of a way you can look at each situation differently? How can you practice being more patient in each circumstance?

- Think of a time when you were impatient for God to answer your prayer, but his reply was "wait." Looking back on the situation now, do you believe God was giving you an opportunity to grow through your patience?

Live It Out

Visit a garden center or nursery with your children. Let them choose a pretty pot and some flower seeds. Once home, plant the seeds and place the pot in a sunny window inside your home. Explain to them that it will take a while before they see any flowers. Have the kids keep a daily journal of the plant's progress. How long does it take for the plant to start sprouting above the soil? How many days until the first flower blooms? Use this project to talk about patience, and that God's timing is perfect for every living thing.

Even More than Daddy

See what great love the Father has lavished on us, that we should be called children of God! And that is what we are! (1 John 3:1)

It's that time of the year again. Santa is back at the mall. (I try hard not to think about how Santa can be in every mall across the country at the very same time, because my mind can only handle so much.)

One year in mid-December, as we were strolling around the mall, we stumbled upon Santa and his elaborate North Pole setup. Since there wasn't a line of kids waiting and we knew that we could get a free candy cane just for stopping by to see him, we decided to do so. My girls took turns sitting on Santa's lap and chatting with him while I pretended to be interested in buying ridiculously-priced photos.

When my girls were done visiting Santa and had received their sweet reward, I asked them what they had asked him to bring them for Christmas. Maile, then 5 years old, replied that she had asked him for a little stuffed dog. This surprised me greatly, because for the last few weeks she had been begging me for a video iPod® (and other similarly expensive gifts) for Christmas. So I asked her about this obvious discrepancy. She smiled up at me from her candy cane and said, "Oh, Daddy! Santa can't get expensive stuff like *that*!"

"Really!" I replied. "But you think that Daddy can?"

"Daddy, you can do *anything*."

In the eyes of my young daughters, no one is bigger, stronger, or smarter than Daddy. Daddy can do anything, fix anything, or be anything. Daddy knows everything there is to know about any topic. But most importantly, they know how much Daddy loves them. I tell them all the time, but I also strive to show them through my actions as well as my words.

It's for these very reasons that blessing my girls during Holy Communion is so important to me. When I'm assisting during a worship service, I have the honor of saying a blessing upon each child who comes forward to the altar with their parents during the Lord's Supper. I usually say something like, "May God bless you today and always, and give you the power to live for Him."

But for my own children, I change it a bit. I simply put my hand on their shoulder and say, "Remember, Jesus loves you even more than Daddy!"

Even more? Is that possible? They know how much Daddy loves them – I won't let them forget! But I feel that it's much more important that they know and understand that Jesus loves them infinitely more than I do. I have to remind them that Daddy is going to make mistakes, and there will be times when he will let you down. Daddy won't know all the answers, and he can't always be there by your side. Try as he might, he won't be able to protect you from everything, and he will fall short of your expectations. Daddy loves you so much – but Jesus loves you so much more, and He will never fail you.

. . . . .

While Christmas is a joyous time of family and friends for many, for others it's the exact opposite. The hurriedness of the season leaves many feeling lonely and worthless. And even though it has become a holiday cliché, this is why we need to remember the true reason for the season. Jesus comforts us in our loneliness, calms our hurriedness with a loving, "**Be still, and know that I am God**" (Psalm 46:10) and reminds us in the manger that He came to start His journey to the cross – because you are worth dying for!

Jesus never fails. He may not always get you what you want – but He gets you what you need. He loves you more than anything, and wants what's best for you.

Have a blessed Christmas season, and always remember how much our heavenly Father loves you!

Pray about It

Dear Jesus,

Thank You for always providing me with the necessities of my life. Thank You for allowing me to provide my family with what they truly need, and more importantly to share with them the love that You have shown me. In turn, help us to share our many blessings with those who are less fortunate, and especially with those who do not yet know You as their Lord and Savior. In Your name I pray, Amen.

Talk about It

- Do your children know that Jesus loves them even more than you love them? How can you remind them of this important truth each day?

- If Jesus truly is "the reason for the season," why do we often push Him aside in our frenzy to buy gifts, decorate our houses, and attend parties? Where does Jesus fall in your priorities this month?

Live It Out

Sometimes in the hurriedness of the Christmas season, we may not notice those around us for whom this time of year is especially difficult. Perhaps they are hurting from a recent loss, or struggling with spiritual emptiness. Identify someone (a neighbor, relative, or coworker) who is experiencing a hard time right now, and invite them to come with you to a Christmas concert or spiritually uplifting event at your church.

Christmas Presents

And there were shepherds living out in the fields nearby, keeping watch over their flocks at night. An angel of the Lord appeared to them, and the glory of the Lord shone around them, and they were terrified. But the angel said to them, "Do not be afraid. I bring you good news that will cause great joy for all the people. Today in the town of David a Savior has been born to you; he is the Messiah, the Lord. This will be a sign to you: You will find a baby wrapped in cloths and lying in a manger." (Luke 2:8-12)

"What do you want for Christmas this year?" I asked Maile in early December. I had noticed that she hadn't brought up the topic recently, which was quite surprising. Normally, right after her birthday in June, she starts working on her Christmas wish list. But here it was, only a few weeks before Christmas, and I hadn't yet heard any gift requests from her.

"Daddy!" Maile scolded me in response. "Christmas isn't just about presents!"

I wish you could have seen my face. I was speechless. And the best part was that she *knew* she had floored me!

. . . . .

Obviously Maile was right – Christmas is certainly not just about the gifts. And if memory serves me correctly, I've had to remind *her* of this quite a few times in the past. Most of us know the real meaning of Christmas. Every December, I notice quite a few people driving around with a bumper sticker on their car that proclaims, "Jesus is the reason for the season!" Yet, all too often, our schedules and priorities in the weeks before Christmas don't accurately reflect that sentiment. Year after year, I'm amazed how the celebration of Jesus' birth seems to get in the way of the *worship* of Jesus. What priority do we give to worship during the Christmas season?

The Church for centuries has set aside the four weeks before Christmas as Advent. Advent is a time of waiting. It's a time of preparation. The word "advent" literally means "coming." Jesus is coming – Christmas is coming – we better get ready. Many churches offer special worship opportunities, and many Advent devotion books exist to help one prepare for the coming time of Christmas. However, even in my short lifetime I'm hearing people talk about or reflect on Advent less and less. Fewer and fewer churches offer special Advent worship services. The ironic thing is that we need Advent now more than ever.

What does your December calendar look like right now? Be honest. Is it filled with parties, get-togethers, shopping excursions, decorating plans, cookie exchanges, and trips to the post office to mail gifts? While there's nothing wrong with any of these activities, they shouldn't overshadow or replace true worship and quiet, humble reflection on the precious gift of our Savior.

Maybe this is the year that Christmas will take on a new focus for you and your family. Maybe this will be the December when worshipping Jesus, not shopping for gifts, will become your top priority. Maybe this is the Advent season when you will truly focus all of your celebration and joy onto the Christ Child, and not onto the pile of gifts under the tree. Maybe you will move the Christmas tree out of the limelight and put the Nativity at the center of your home – and your heart.

My favorite characters in the Nativity story have always been the shepherds. I played a shepherd several times in church Christmas pageants. To me, the shepherds are the most relatable. The wise men, Mary and Joseph, angels, the innkeeper – all great characters. But there's something about the shepherds. They were just out doing their thing, living their lives when all of a sudden – they were invited to the party (and rumor has it that shepherds didn't get invited to a whole lot of parties!) by an army of angels. They got to be some of the first to experience baby Jesus. They dropped everything and went off to see Jesus (Luke 2:13-20).

My prayer for all of us this holiday season is that the same Christmas Spirit that captured the shepherds in Luke 2:20, which caused them to glorify and praise God for all they had seen and heard, will capture us! You've been invited to the party – it's time to experience Jesus this Christmas season!

Pray about It

Dear Jesus,
   You should be the focus of my mind and heart every day, but especially during Advent! Let Your Holy Spirit motivate my family to pay less attention to earthly festivities this Christmas season, and to focus on celebrating and giving thanks for the most glorious gift of all – Your birth! In Your name I pray, Amen.

Talk about It

- Do you and your family truly enjoy the celebration of Advent, or do you tend to get busy with more secular "holiday" activities and events?

- How can you use your spiritual gifts to help others experience Jesus in a whole new way this Christmas season?

Live It Out

Buy or borrow an Advent devotional book to use in your daily prayer time with God. Look for one that you can read aloud together as a family. Reading these devotions will help you set your hearts and minds on the coming of Christ. Also, if your church offers midweek Advent services, make a commitment to attend them together as part of your celebrations this season.

A New Year

Therefore, if anyone is in Christ, the new creation has come: The old has gone, the new is here! (2 Corinthians 5:17)

On December 31st, 2009, Maile decided she was going to stay up until midnight to celebrate New Year's Eve. Since she was six and a half years old and full of will power, we figured she just might be able to make it.

So, as we prepared to go to a New Year's Eve party at the home of our friends, Leilani put on her pajamas (she knew *she* wasn't going to make it!) and Maile dressed up in her fanciest party clothes – ready for a night of fun.

It was a great evening. The adults talked and laughed while the kids watched a movie. Everyone gathered together for a time of sharing favorite memories and blessings of the past year. We even sang some songs. As it grew later in the evening, I asked Maile several times how she was doing, and each time she replied, "Great!"

Right before midnight, we passed out some glasses with champagne and sparkling cider. Then the countdown began: "10, 9, 8, 7, 6, 5, 4, 3, 2, 1 – HAPPY NEW YEAR!" I congratulated Maile for staying awake all the way until midnight. We kissed, made a few toasts with our glasses, and then very quickly packed up to head home.

As we said our good-byes and started heading out the door, Maile's face changed rapidly from joy to confusion, and then to great disappointment. She stopped in the doorway, arms crossed. "WAIT!" she demanded. "That's it?!?"

I put my arm around her, smiling. "Yes honey, that's it. Time to go home now and get some sleep."

Maile had thought something magical was sure to happen after the clock ticked over into the brand-new year. She had expected some sort of transformation at midnight. Instead, everything – and everyone – seemed to be exactly the same at 12:00 midnight as they were at 11:59 p.m.

. . . . .

Most of the big changes and defining moments in our lives probably don't occur just because we flip the calendar over to a new page. But New Year's celebrations are a great reminder of the new opportunities that every year provides for us. Most of us, in fact, enjoy the feeling of starting over with a "clean slate." We might even make a list of resolutions to further our goals and break us from our bad habits.

Of course, there's nothing really magical about January 1st. The truth is that every moment of every day is a brand-new opportunity for change and growth. God wants to work in our hearts each day to strengthen us, heal us, and renew us. No matter what has happened in the past, or what mistakes we have made, we can always be confident that better things are in store for us! 2 Corinthians 5:17 reassures us that through God's incredible love in Christ Jesus, we are given a new beginning! The old has passed away, and we are new creations. We can start anew, having been forgiven and redeemed.

What are you going to do with your 365 brand-new days? Take your family on a vacation of a lifetime? Invite your neighbor to church? Feed a hungry family? Sign up for a mission trip? Challenge yourself to do something that is so significant, so life-giving and extraordinary, that you will never look back at the end of the year, confused and disappointed, and say, "Wait! That's it?!?"

Pray about It

Dear Father,
Thank You for the blessing of this new day, and for every day to come. Each day, You give me so many brand-new opportunities to share Your love with others. Please forgive me when I fail to make the most of the days You have so graciously allotted to me on this earth. Help me to use each one to serve You, always bringing You glory in everything I do. In Jesus' name, Amen.

Talk about It

- Have you made a list of New Year's resolutions? If so, what changes do you want to make in your life for this brand-new year? In particular, what goals would you like to set to further enrich and strengthen your spiritual life?

- Satan often tries to trick us into believing that we are stuck in our sins and failures, and that there is no new beginning. Why does he want us to believe that we can't start over?

Live It Out

As a family, take some time together to reflect back over the past twelve months. Talk about the high points and low points, and all the blessings and frustrations you experienced. Write down a list of things you regret not doing in the past twelve months. What can you do differently this coming year to fulfill more of your goals, dreams, and priorities?

Happy

"Though I am free and belong to no one, I have made myself a slave to everyone, to win as many as possible. To the Jews I became like a Jew, to win the Jews. To those under the law I became like one under the law (though I myself am not under the law), so as to win those under the law. To those not having the law I became like one not having the law (though I am not free from God's law but am under Christ's law), so as to win those not having the law. To the weak I became weak, to win the weak. I have become all things to all people so that by all possible means I might save some. I do all this for the sake of the gospel, that I may share in its blessings." (1 Corinthians 9:19-23)

Back when Maile was in kindergarten, the teacher selected one child every Monday to be "Student of the Week." There were many special rights and privileges reserved for the honoree. Maile could barely wait until it was her special week. As part of the celebration, she was asked to bring in a treat to share with everyone in the class. Maile was very excited about sharing a snack with her friends, and asked me for ideas of what to bring. I suggested all of her favorites: cookies, cupcakes, ice cream, crispy rice treats, etc. But each time I made a suggestion, she quickly informed me of someone in her class who wouldn't like it. (Someone actually dislikes chocolate ice cream?)

After a while, I ran out of ideas. Wow, this was certainly a picky bunch of kids! Maile looked discouraged, so finally I shared some of my fatherly wisdom with her.

"You know, honey," I said, "You can't always make everyone happy."

Maile looked me right in the eyes and asked, "Why not?"

· · · · ·

It's a good question, isn't it? Why *can't* we make everyone happy? I guess I've never really spent much time thinking about this one. I just accept it as a fact. Everyone is different, after all. Everyone has different likes and dislikes, different backgrounds, and different experiences. In most groups I've observed or been a part of, it has been difficult (if not impossible) to please everyone.

Even Jesus couldn't make everyone happy. In fact, He made people so upset that they killed Him. It's hard for us to imagine how anyone could have been so upset with Jesus that they would put Him to death. But even though He had healed the blind and the sick, fed the multitudes, performed many miracles, and forgave the sins of the people, apparently this still wasn't enough to make everyone happy. Jesus was still scorned, hated, and rejected.

St. Paul writes in 1 Corinthians 9, "**I have become all things to all people so that by all possible means I might save some.**" Paul is saying that he is willing to go to great lengths to have the gospel message resonate with the various people he comes in contact with, so that as many people as possible might come to faith by the power of the Holy Spirit. Paul wants everyone to know and understand God's passionate, everlasting love. But the reality is that human beings rebel, even against such a powerful and saving love. They don't believe it; they don't trust it. They think that they don't need it, and they don't even want it in their lives.

Jesus was rejected when He came to earth and walked in human flesh. He is still being rejected by so many people today, even as He sits on His throne in heaven. And yet, Jesus **"wants all people to be saved and to come to a knowledge of the truth"** (1 Timothy 2:4). He longs to bless and bring joy to each one of us through the forgiveness of sins and the promise of everlasting life.

Today, Christians are not always known for being happy, joyful people. But 2,000 years ago when the church was just getting started, people wanted to join because they were amazed at how the people loved each other (cf. Acts 2:44-47). Conditions were hard and people were being martyred – but somehow they still found joy this side of heaven. Maybe they were able to be truly happy because they knew that heaven was their inheritance. Maybe they found joy in unconditionally loving other people. Maybe the knowledge of salvation sustained their hope. Maybe all of the above.

These early Christians clearly demonstrated that true joy comes from remaining in Christ's love (cf. John 15:10-12), not from chasing after the whims of the world – on the one hand ignoring God's blessings and on the other hand being quick to blame God for any bumps in the road. As Christians today, our contrasting behavior in the light of seemingly adverse events can be a powerful witness to those God has placed in our lives, especially when a bond of trust has been formed. No, our witness won't make everyone happy, but a few may be blessed. May God give us the opportunities and the courage to share His love with others in this way.

Pray about It

Dear Father,

Thank You for my happiness – in knowing that You sent Your Son Jesus to die on the cross for the sins of the world, so that we may one day spend eternity in heaven with You! God, forgive me when I don't spread that joyful news with non-Christians out of fear that the message might not please them. Give me the courage and motivation to spread the joy of Your love with great contagiousness! I pray this in Jesus' name, Amen.

Talk about It

- What specific things or people in your life do you credit with being responsible for most of your happiness (or lack thereof)? In considering these things, do you think you invest your happiness wisely?

- We won't always be happy in this life, and although it is unrealistic to expect to be continually happy, Scripture talks of an undying joy that accompanies our walk with Jesus. What is the difference between this type of joy, and temporary happiness?

Live It Out

Think of some small but meaningful ways in which you can share the happiness you have in Christ with someone else each day. Perhaps an encouraging note, a smile, a small gift, or a thoughtful gesture? Look for all the big and little opportunities that God provides for you to share His joy.

Missing

*"The LORD himself goes before you and will be with you;
he will never leave you nor forsake you. Do not be afraid;
do not be discouraged."* (Deuteronomy 31:8)

Nothing good happens after midnight. At least that's what my
high school football coach said at the end of every Friday
practice and Saturday post-game speech. And my friends who
serve in the military have told me that the perfect time to
attack the enemy in modern warfare is at 4 a.m. – a whole 4
hours after midnight! It is believed that 4 a.m. is the time
when even the wildest partiers are heading to bed (or at least
unable to make much of a resistance) and it's before the time
when even the earliest morning risers arise.

So, of course, at exactly 4 a.m. one night, Maile ran into our
bedroom, tears streaming down her cheeks, crying hyster-
ically. She tried to speak but I couldn't make sense out of
what she was trying to tell me. Finally she managed to
sputter, "I… can't… find… Leilani!"

Faster than a speeding bullet, I jumped out of bed. I didn't
want to be the father who lost fifty percent of his offspring.
Completely panicked, I darted into her room, frantically
looking everywhere for her – or for clues to where she might
be. Had she fallen off the bed? Was she sleepwalking? Did
my four-year-old run away? Was she kidnapped? A thousand

confused and frightened thoughts ran through my mind as I tried to sleepily process what was happening.

I quickly ran through the rest of the house, my eyes searching everywhere for my precious little one. Not in the kitchen. Not in the bathroom. Not curled up on the living room sofa. My stomach felt sick. "Where is she?!" I cried out in desperation.

When I ran back into Leilani's room again, I "found" her. She was sleeping soundly in her bed, right where she belonged – but of course it was the last place I had looked. Poor Maile had merely dreamed that her sister was missing – but in reality, she wasn't. Leilani had been right there in bed the whole time, fast asleep. She was right where she was supposed to be, and in my panic, I hadn't even seen her there.

· · · · ·

How often do we wonder where God is? We see the painful tragedies and difficulties happening in the world around us, as well as the ones we experience in our own lives, and we don't understand. How could He let that hurricane kill all of those people and ruin so many lives? How could God allow my husband to get cancer? Why doesn't God help me find a job? Doesn't he care that my child is sick, my marriage is on the rocks, and I'm struggling to make ends meet? Life is so unpredictable and disorienting. There is so much pain to be found. In our panic and confusion, we sometimes run around searching for what is right in front of us. Confused and hurt, we cry out, "Where is God?"

God is right where He has promised to be – He is here with us, through everything we face on earth. He unconditionally and eternally loves a broken world, flooding our lives with His mercy and compassion, and forgiving all of our sins. He promises that He will never leave us nor forsake us (Deuteronomy 31:8). And He rejoices in the day when He will bring us to heaven with Him, to live eternally where there is no more sin, or tragedies, or hurting, or pain.

Knowing God is with us gives us peace – a peace that passes all human understanding, creativity, ingenuity, knowledge, wisdom, and know-how. While we often don't understand God's ways, with this peace in our lives, we can get through anything!

Pray about It

Dear Father,

Thank You for Your continual presence in my life. I am blessed to have the comforting knowledge that You are always with me – in the best times as well as the worst. Let the Holy Spirit open my eyes and my heart to see You in the places and people where it might seem like You are "missing." And allow me to show You to others who are still seeking You. I pray this in Jesus' name, Amen.

Talk about It

- Think of a time when you wondered or doubted whether God was truly there with you. What circumstances led you to feel as if God wasn't there? What helped you to realize that He was still right there beside you?

- Sometimes we have the feeling that something is missing in our lives, but we aren't quite sure what it is. What

things might be missing from your life right now? What
can you pray for?

Live It Out

Think of someone you know who's going through a really
difficult time right now – someone who may have trouble
seeing God's presence through their struggles and pain. Invite
them out for coffee, call them on the phone, or send them an
e-mail. Let them know you are there to listen and help in any
way. Pray for the best words to say to comfort them and help
them see that God is truly with them and loves them.

What Do You Do?

But you are a chosen people, a royal priesthood, a holy nation, God's special possession, that you may declare the praises of him who called you out of darkness into his wonderful light. Once you were not a people, but now you are the people of God; once you had not received mercy, but now you have received mercy. (1 Peter 2:9-10)

"What do you do?"

It's one of the most common questions we ask when we meet someone. It seems like a simple question at first. But is it really? Do we really want our job/occupation/career to be the definitive descriptor of who we are?

"What do you do?" is one of those questions that can lead to long, fascinating conversations and new friendships – or it can lead to an awkward excuse to move on to talk to someone else. Being in ministry, I've noticed that when new people find out what I do for a living, they either have a ton of questions for me or no longer want to talk to me. These encounters are most fascinating when on an airplane where my seatmate and I know we'll be spending quite a bit of time together. Sometimes we'll end up talking the entire trip about the nuances of theology, and other times complete silence follows my answer. Sometimes I don't even get to ask the question back!

One afternoon, while we were at a church gathering, everyone was taking turns going around the circle and sharing who they are and what they do for a living. It was an intergenerational group, so the answers were quite varied: "college student," "dentist," "retired businessman," "stay-at-home mom," etc.

When it was Leilani's turn, my preschooler proudly announced, "Hi, I'm Leilani, and my job is to tell people about Jesus!"

There was a momentary pause as everyone stopped and looked at her with wide eyes. Their initial shock quickly turned to smiles and affirmations. They could see that even at the young age of five years old, Leilani understood that the job of all followers of Jesus is to tell people about Him. It doesn't matter whether or not we hold an official paid position in the church. As Christians, it is our job to proclaim Christ. It's what we do.

· · · · ·

St. Peter reminds us in 1 Peter 2 that we are a royal priesthood. That sounds quite impressive! Are you putting that on your resume? What does royal priesthood even mean? Kings and Priests. When you look back at history, you'll learn that these two groups often didn't get along. There tended to be power struggles between the two groups as everyone fought for their own selfish gain.

Priests were the ones who had a special connection to God. And Jesus came to give *everyone* that "connection." The temple curtain, that acted as a partition between the area only the priests could enter and a more common area, was torn in half at the moment Jesus died (Matthew 27:50-51). Jesus is our King – but we are welcomed into His royal family through His death and resurrection. You have the rights and privileges of the royals and the priests!

We are called to share Jesus' love with the world. We don't have to be employed professionally as a pastor, or a Director of Christian Education, to be in ministry. In fact, the "amateur" ministers among us can be the most effective of all! People expect a pastor to talk about Jesus – but not the butcher, the baker, or the candlestick maker. Whatever your vocation may be, you can reach people right where you already are. And when you do, it can open hearts and minds in ways that ministry "professionals" can't.

Your witness doesn't have to include complex scriptural orations. Your kindness, compassion, love, generosity, work ethic, patience, goodness, and self control communicate Jesus in very effective ways. Every interaction with another human being is a chance to use that "royal priesthood" title.

It's every believer's responsibility to tell people about Jesus. What are you doing to share Him with others?

Pray about It

Dear Jesus,

Help me to remember that the most important job I will ever have is to share You with the world. Let the Holy Spirit work in my heart to compel me to tell people – at work, at church, even on an airplane! – all about Your incredible love for us. Thank You for all the roles You have given me in my life, and for the promise of an eternity with You in heaven! I pray these things in Your name, Amen.

Talk about It

- It is easy for us to get so caught up in our busy lives that we forget about our most important occupation – being Jesus' disciple! Can you think of something that you can do *today* that will help further your mission of sharing Jesus with those around you?

- What specific, God-given abilities do you possess that could benefit and bless the people around you? How can you use these gifts to point others to Jesus?

Live It Out

Share your "Royal Priesthood" title with someone this week. You don't have to tell them about it directly, but take some time to mention to someone you meet that you love Jesus. Tell them about what He has done in your life. Invite them to come with you to church and hear what your royal priesthood is all about.

Spending Time with Daddy

And let us consider how we may spur one another on toward love and good deeds, not giving up meeting together, as some are in the habit of doing, but encouraging one another – and all the more as you see the Day approaching.
(Hebrews 10:24-25)

One of the perks of living in Orange County, CA is that Disneyland is close by. During the years we spent living in Southern California, we were fortunate enough to have annual passes to the park, which meant that we took the girls fairly often. They never seemed to tire of going; there was always a new experience waiting for them. The girls looked forward to going each and every time.

I remember one Saturday in particular when I had promised to take the girls to Disneyland for the whole day. However, Maile woke up sick that morning and had to stay home. Since Leilani was still looking forward to going, I decided to take her – just the two of us. We had lots of fun. I let Leilani choose all of the rides and shows. We ate wherever she wanted to eat. She had my undivided attention the entire day. And just as the day was about to turn to night and our special time together was nearing its end, Leilani turned to me and said, "Daddy, I miss Maile."

"Really?" I asked, surprised. "I thought you'd be happy having Daddy all to yourself today."

"I liked it a lot, Daddy," she explained, "but some things are just so much more fun when Maile is with us too."

That's a pretty sweet sentiment, especially coming from a little sister who is often picked on, bossed around, and left out of things. But what struck me about Leilani's comment was that I remembered a previous afternoon when Maile had also been sick. Leilani had just gotten a little Barbie golf club set for Christmas, so the two of us went to the driving range to hit golf balls. About halfway through our golfing time together, Leilani said, "Daddy, this is so much more fun without Maile! I'm glad it's just you and me today!"

Now maybe she was just having a difficult day with her sister. It wouldn't be the first time, and it certainly won't be the last. Or maybe there's something deeper going on here. Maybe there are times when we need to be alone with our Daddy, and then there are other times when we need to be in community with our Daddy.

. . . . .

It's the same in our spiritual lives as well. We need the intimate times when we are alone with God – talking, praying, listening, praising, reading His Word, and building our relationship (cf. Matthew 14:23). But there are also times when we need to be in corporate worship with our heavenly Father. Being a part of a larger body of believers reminds us that God is so much bigger than us and our little "bubble." It reinforces and strengthens our faith when we spend time with others who share our beliefs (cf. Acts 2:46-47).

We need both types of time with our heavenly Father, and yet sometimes we let things get out of balance in our spiritual lives. Maybe we've been reading our Bible regularly at home and have an active prayer life but, for whatever reason, we haven't attended a worship service in a few months. Or perhaps we've been faithful in our church attendance, but our prayer and devotional time at home has fallen by the wayside. There may even be times when we neglect both personal and corporate time with God. Our schedules get busy and before we know it, our special times with God have been compromised and left behind. God wants us to keep a healthy balance in our lives which includes both one-on-one time with our Father as well as group Bible study and worship.

How is the spiritual balance in your life right now? Are you making time for prayer and devotional reading in the quiet moments of your day? When Sunday morning rolls around, are you lying on the couch or praising God in the pews? Do you need to make some changes in your priorities? God is waiting to spend some quality time with you!

Pray about It

Dear Father,

Thank You for the different opportunities You have given me to praise and worship You, and for the people You have placed in my life to share those times with. Help me to prioritize and balance my daily life so that I spend enough time with You alone as well as with a group of other believers. I pray this in Jesus' name, Amen.

Talk about It

- Some people feel that, because "God is everywhere," there is no real need to attend church or experience corporate worship. What would you say to such a person concerning the joys and blessings that they are missing out on?

- Are you giving equal priority to your personal and corporate time with God? If not, what could you do differently to create more balance between the two?

Live It Out

Who do you need to spend some quality time with? Maybe it's someone you haven't connected with in a while, or perhaps it is your own spouse or child. Sit down with a calendar and plan some special activities with your loved one. Go out for lunch at their favorite restaurant. Spend the day (or even an hour or two) working on a project or craft together. Have a picnic in the park. Take a long walk and just listen to whatever they wish to talk about. Conclude your time together by planning another activity to do soon.

Confession

If we claim to be without sin, we deceive ourselves and the truth is not in us. If we confess our sins, he is faithful and just and will forgive us our sins and purify us from all unrighteousness. (1 John 1:8-9)

I think that every parent can name at least one game that their child absolutely adores, but that they themselves could easily do without. Old Maid has always been one of Maile's favorite card games, but I have to admit that it is definitely my least favorite. Now, don't get me wrong – I adore playing games with my girls! I am always grateful for the time we are able to spend together, having fun and building memories. But I've always found myself groaning inwardly every time Maile pulls out that deck of Old Maid cards. Oh, joy!

One day, it finally dawned on me why I dislike this particular game so much. *I never won!* I've always been a person with a fairly competitive nature, and my losing streak at Old Maid drove me crazy. Why couldn't I ever win this stupid game?

I don't remember exactly when it happened, but one day as Maile and I were playing the game, I finally figured out why I had never been able to win. Maile had secretly marked the Old Maid card! She always knew which one it was! And here, all this time, I just thought that she was incredibly skilled at cards, and that maybe she would be able to "go pro" with her Old Maid skills someday. I had envisioned her winning tournaments and bringing home the big prize money – and taking care of Daddy in the way he deserves to be treated. Needless to say, her card-marking scheme was quite a shock to me.

When I confronted Maile about her cheating, at first she denied it. She insisted she hadn't done anything, and claimed to have no idea what I was talking about. But after a lengthy interrogation, she finally broke down and admitted that yes, she had marked the card. When I asked her why she would cheat, and then make matters worse by lying about it, she replied, "But I like to win, Daddy!"

Whenever I need to discipline my daughters, I always try to talk them through the process of confession. First, I ask them to tell me truthfully what happened. Then I explain why it was a wrong choice to make, and show them passages in the Bible where God has instructed us to behave otherwise. I explain the consequences of their misbehavior, and whatever punishment they will have. And then I proclaim God's forgiveness and love – and mine.

After they confess their sin to me, I always ask them, "Honey, doesn't it feel good to tell me this?" It usually does! They experience a great sense of relief from confessing their sin and receiving forgiveness. I want them to associate this "feeling" with the process of confession and absolution. Hopefully it brings the head knowledge and the heart knowledge together. Confession is tough. It's hard on our pride to admit that we screwed up. Sometimes there are serious consequences for our actions, and we have to pay a price for them. But confession always sets us free – and being free is an amazing feeling!

Not long after the Old Maid card-marking incident, there came a day when it was my turn to ask for forgiveness. I had broken a promise to Leilani, who was four years old at the time. I pulled her aside, held her in my arms, and confessed my broken promise. Then I apologized for hurting her, and expressed my need for forgiveness. Having been on the other end of this event many times, Leilani squeezed me tightly, looked me in the eyes and asked, "Daddy, doesn't it feel good to tell me this?" Yes, it did feel good! In fact, it felt great!

· · · · ·

We all have a deep spiritual need to confront and work through our sins, mistakes, and issues. Although we were born sinful in a fallen world, God created us to do good. Sin separates us from our Father, and although we need to make things right with Him, we cannot do it ourselves. Jesus gave His life in our place so that we now have forgiveness for our mistakes and rebellion, and reconciliation with God once again.

The apostle John explains it this way: "**If we confess our sins, he is faithful and just and will forgive us our sins and purify us from all unrighteousness.**" (1 John 1:9) Confession is an important part of forgiveness and restoration. Jesus is faithful, but He is also just. Sin is no laughing matter; it's serious business, and it needs to be dealt with. But once we confess our shortcomings and failures, and lay all of our shame, guilt, and sin at the foot of the cross, the promise is clear: we will be forgiven and we will be made pure. Our Father's love and mercy is greater than we can ever fathom. That sure feels good!

Pray about It

Dear Father,
   I confess that I have disobeyed and sinned against You
many times over today. Thank You for allowing me to approach You even while I am heavy laden with shame and
guilt. Thank You for loving me so much that You sacrificed
Your Son on the cross to pay the price for my sinfulness. I
am now forgiven, cleansed, and set free because of what
Jesus has done for me. What a precious gift! In Jesus' name I
pray, Amen.

Talk about It

- Do you find yourself admitting your sin to others only
  after you've already been caught? Why is it so difficult
  for us to readily confess our wrongdoing to others? What
  are we afraid of?

- How do you respond when your child confesses his or
  her sin to you? Do you tend to focus solely on the
  wrongdoing? Do you remember to share God's forgiveness (and your own) with the guilty party?

Live It Out

Most of us still carry around a hurtful injustice or painful
incident from our past. Perhaps it was a friend who betrayed
us, or a parent who wasn't there for us when we were
growing up. Set aside time this week to sit down and write
out a letter of forgiveness to that person. This letter doesn't
need to be sent or seen by anyone else – this can be for you

alone. By proclaiming your forgiveness and God's, you may begin to experience freedom and relief from some of the hurt and pain which you have carried around inside your heart.

Spring

114

Play Ball!

I am the gate; whoever enters through me will be saved. They will come in and go out, and find pasture. The thief comes only to steal and kill and destroy; I have come that they may have life, and have it to the full. (John 10:9-10)

I love this time of year. It's time for Spring Training and the start of another glorious baseball season! I'm a sports nut, but baseball is by far my favorite, and it always has been. I remember watching the games on TV and keeping score even as a little kid. I still have shoeboxes filled with old baseball cards. Some say baseball is an acquired taste, and if that's true, well, I just might be addicted! Every time I hear the conclusion of the National Anthem, I feel the need to yell, "Play ball!"

Before Christy and I had kids, I remember going to ball games and watching fathers explain all the ins and outs of baseball to their kids. They were literally passing down the love of the game to their children, and it was so beautiful to behold. I told Christy that nothing made me want to be a father more than watching these loving fathers share their baseball knowledge with their offspring. She laughed and thought I was joking. But I wasn't!

When God blessed us with children, I couldn't wait to take them to a ball game. Maile's very first ball game was in August of 2003. She was 2 months old and it was

"Thunderstick Night" at Angel Stadium. Not a good venue for an infant! Needless to say, it wasn't the memorable experience of daddy-daughter bonding that I had dreamed of. Christy spend the whole game in the women's restroom, trying to calm a screaming baby. She made it very clear, in a way that only a wife can, that it would be quite a while before she and Maile would be attending another baseball game.

Flash forward to a beautiful spring day, several years later. Maile was now at the ripe, influential age of 3. She knew of her father's incredible love for baseball, and I felt the time was right for a do-over of her very first game. We talked it up for days in advance. We could all feel the anticipation and excitement building. This was going to be the best time of our lives! And when the big day finally arrived, Maile was dressed up in baseball clothes. She wore a baseball cap and brought her baseball glove. She was ready for a memorable experience!

We arrived at the stadium and I was bursting with excitement, anxious to start teaching her all the intricate nuances of the game. My passion for this beautiful sport was going to be passed down through the generations! Maile even paid attention to the game – for about half an inning, anyway – and then she dropped the ultimate question.

"Um, Daddy, when do WE get to play?"

Confused, I replied, "Maile, we don't play baseball here. We come to watch the baseball players play."

Even more confused, Maile then asked, "Why would we want to just sit here and watch *other* people play?"

At that point, I couldn't really do anything but laugh. It was a little painful at first, but I laughed anyway. I guess if you really think about it, it *is* kind of silly to just sit and watch other people play.

. . . . .

Like the saying goes, life is not a spectator sport. It isn't about sitting and watching. It's about going out there on the field and playing. It's about doing the most with whatever we've got. Jesus says in John 10:10 that He came to earth so that we might have life, and have it to the full. The "full" is about getting involved, and making a difference in people's lives. It's about having proper priorities and actually living out those priorities – not just talking about them. A full life in Christ is about playing, not watching!

Jackie Robinson, the first African-American to play Major League Baseball, said it like this: "A life is not important except in the impact it has on other lives." Impact comes from getting involved, not from sitting on the bleachers. So, with the freshness of spring in the air, how are you going to impact the lives of others? Let's play ball!

Pray about It

Dear Jesus,
    I pray that I will learn from and be motivated by the positive influences of other strong and faithful Christians around me. But most of all, Lord, lead me by Your own holy and perfect example. Strengthen my courage so that I will get out of the stands and onto the playing field, where others can witness Your mercy and love through my actions. In Your name I pray, Amen.

Talk about It

- We are called to experience life to the "full." (cf. John 10:10) What does that mean to you and your family? How can you have a "full" experience in your daily walk with Christ?

- Many aspects of our lives were shaped and developed by the experiences we had as children. What kind of spiritual influence did your family have on you as a child? What kinds of positive spiritual experiences are you now having with your own children?

Live It Out

Think of an area of your spiritual life in which you are more of a spectator than a player. Maybe you don't attend church regularly, or have never been part of a Bible study class. Perhaps you've never read the Bible in its entirety. Challenge yourself to add something new and different to your life that will help you grow closer to God. Even better – find a friend to join you in this activity. Get off the bleachers and into the game!

The Scooter

I cry aloud to the LORD;
I lift up my voice to the LORD for mercy.
I pour out before him my complaint;
before him I tell my trouble. (Psalm 142:1-2)

Not long ago, Maile decided that she really wanted a Razor®
Scooter. Every time she would bring up the topic, I would
lovingly respond, "Sure, honey – just save your money."

She did. She got the brightest pink scooter that money could
buy. Maile loved her new scooter and rode it all over the
neighborhood. We live in Texas "Hill Country," so on a
scooter, the streets can feel like a roller coaster. She loved it!

One afternoon, Maile was riding her scooter ahead of me as I
walked down to the store. She was going pretty fast on a
downhill stretch, and was maybe 30 feet in front of me when
she suddenly hit a bump in the sidewalk. I can still see this
part in my mind in slow motion. She went flying, head first. It
was like a stone skipping across a pond. It happened so fast,
and there was nothing I could do to stop it. I ran to pick her
up off the ground – and let me tell you, the ground had won.
She had a big scrape on the side of her face. Her knees and
elbows were all scratched up. She was a mess.

But Maile didn't shed one tear. I hugged her tightly and asked
her if she was okay, and she bravely replied, "I'm fine." She

was shaking as she told me this, but she refused to cry. I wondered if she knew that I didn't believe that she was fine, but since she wanted to play tough, I was going to let her.

"Maile," I asked, "Can I hold your scooter while we walk home?"

"No," she insisted, stone-faced and still shaking, "I'm going to ride it."

After riding her scooter a few feet, she stopped and asked me, "Daddy? Can you hold my scooter?"

"Of course, honey, I'd be happy to. Do you want me to carry you too?"

"No thanks. I'm going to walk."

She limped along, refusing to let me even hold her hand. She was cradling her left arm as well, which was all scraped up and obviously hurt a great deal. She was trying so hard to be tough, and while a part of me was proud of her, an even bigger part of me longed for her to let me hold her in my arms. I wanted to comfort her and do whatever I could to make her feel better. But it's hard to provide comfort to someone who won't admit that they need it.

When we finally got home, Leilani ran into the living room to greet us. She took one look at her big sister's scraped limbs and screamed, "That's gotta hurt!" Little sisters know how to tell it like it is!

Maile still kept her composure, determined to keep up her courageous front – until Mommy walked in the room and saw her bleeding and injured. All Mommy had to do was to say

"Awww..." in that sweet Mommy way, and then the flood-gates opened. The tears poured out, and Maile cried like she has never cried before. Mommy picked her up, held her tenderly, and took her upstairs to start cleansing all of the wounds.

I wish Maile would have cried out to me. I wish she hadn't been so stubborn and would have let me help her. It was so painful to watch her hurting – and the pain grew with every step, because I knew I could easily help her and comfort her. But she refused.

. . . . .

Our heavenly Father longs for us to cry out to Him. The writer of Psalm 142 says in verses 5-6: "**I cry to you, LORD; I say, 'You are my refuge, my portion in the land of the living.' Listen to my cry, for I am in desperate need; rescue me from those who pursue me, for they are too strong for me.**" It pains God when we try to go it alone. He created us to be in a close relationship with Him. There is nothing too big for Him to handle – and He *wants* to handle it! But all too often, we put on our brave facade and insist that we don't need His help. He won't force Himself upon us; He lets us choose whether to come to Him with our pain and hurt, or to suffer alone in silence.

Is there something you long to cry out about? Are you being stubborn and trying to handle it by yourself? Remember that He is there beside you in your pain. Let God put His arms around you and comfort you. He longs to give you His strength and His peace. Hold God to His promise to listen. Weeping, sorrow, pain, loneliness, laughter, joy – Jesus experienced it all during his 33 years on earth. Besides wanting us to cry out to Him and promising to listen, He also understands.

Remember one of Jesus' last words from the cross? "**My God, my God, why have you forsaken me?**" (Matthew 27:46) He understands in ways that we will never comprehend. And as our Lord hung on that cross, He knew to cry out to His Father. We can take comfort in knowing that our heavenly Father also responds to our cries.

Pray about It

Dear Father,
   Too often I try to handle everything myself unnecessarily. I don't always cry out to You in times of pain or need, even though I know You are waiting to hold me in Your arms and comfort me. Please help me to put aside my pride and come to You. Thank You for always listening to my prayers and requests – spoken or unspoken – and for comforting my troubled heart and mind. I pray this in the name of Your Son Jesus Christ, Amen.

Talk about It

- Why is it so frustrating when someone we love is obviously hurting but won't allow us to help? Should we still try to reach out to someone who doesn't want our help?

- What problems, anxieties, and troubles are you trying to handle by yourself? What is holding you back from crying out to God for comfort?

Live It Out

Think of someone you know who is struggling with emotional or physical challenges. What are some ways you can let this person know that you care about the difficulties they are facing, and that you are there to listen and provide comfort? Ask God to provide you with opportunities to show Christ's love to this person in tangible ways.

Heartbreak

From noon until three in the afternoon darkness came over all the land. About three in the afternoon Jesus cried out in a loud voice, "Eli, Eli, lema sabachthani?" (which means "My God, my God, why have you forsaken me?"). (Matthew 27:45-46)

There is nothing quite like the heartache of watching your child in pain. I would much rather be in ten times more pain myself than to watch either of my kids go through it. Perhaps the hardest part is the helplessness that we, as parents, feel. We know that as much as we might try, we can't always alleviate the pain or fix what's wrong. We try so hard to clear an easy path for our kids, and to make their lives as easy and smooth as possible. But we can't shelter them from every bump and bruise – and there still will be times when things will hurt.

When our daughter Maile was a baby, she was very small for her age. For a while, she was ranked in the "zero percentile" on the growth chart at the pediatrician's office. Basically, this meant that nearly 100% of children her age were bigger than she was. To me, she didn't really look any smaller than other kids. But what did I know? Aren't babies supposed to be small?

By the time Maile reached the age of eighteen months, the doctors wanted to do a biopsy on her to see if she was allergic to wheat, which may have explained why she was so small. Of course, as life would have it, the test was scheduled for two days after Leilani was born. Daddy and Maile were arriving at the hospital to check in just as Mommy and the new baby were checking out to go home. I was a bit nervous about taking a toddler to be prodded and poked by medical staff without the reassuring presence and experienced hands of Mommy along with us. But I kept telling myself, "What could go wrong?"

Everything started out just fine. The nurse gave little Maile a stuffed octopus to cuddle, and she was delighted. They put us in the nice private room to watch TV. For a while, it didn't seem bad at all.

But once the nurse walked in and announced that it was time to put a needle in Maile's arm, all *you-know-what* broke loose. Maile fidgeted and whined, which soon escalated into crying and screaming. She made it quite clear that this was all happening completely against her will. The nurse called for backup, and it took several people to hold her still so they could insert the needle into her arm. Then, just as I started to reassure Maile that it was almost over, the nurse interrupted me and explained that they would need to leave the needle in so they could administer the anesthesia. As she left the room, she smiled at Maile kindly and said, "I'll be right back."

I'm not sure what "right back" means to you, but I was assuming it meant a few seconds – maybe as long as a minute. I mean, my eighteen month old daughter had a needle sticking out of her arm! They wouldn't leave me alone with her for very long, right? Wrong. The nurse came back into the room 45 minutes later. By that point, I had almost lost the ability to hear from all of the screaming. But the worst part of the waiting period was not the noise, or the tears, or the fear of dropping her as she wrestled in my arms trying to break free. The most difficult part was seeing the painful look in her eyes. She would look deeply into my eyes and just scream, "Da-a-a-a-d-d-dy!" It was absolutely heartbreaking.

I don't think I've ever felt more helpless. I knew I could help her. I could rip the needle out – knock over a few nurses – and be out the door before security knew what had happened. I could make the pain stop. But that wasn't the best thing for her. The best thing for her was the painful needle staying in her arm until we figured out what, if anything, was wrong. I had to look at the bigger picture of a needle actually doing some good.

· · · · ·

We may not have given much thought to the heartbreak that our heavenly Father must have felt when His one and only Son hung on the cross and cried out, "**My God, my God, why have you forsaken me?**" (Matthew 27:46) Surely this must have been incredibly difficult to watch! There is no pain like seeing your child suffering. Surely God the Father could have rescued Jesus from the suffering He endured (cf. Luke 4:10) – but the world needed a Savior. There had to be a death for there to be a resurrection.

Just prior to the well-known account of Noah's Ark, we are told that God "grieved," (Genesis 6:6; King James version), and then it rained for forty days and nights. Was God crying? I believe that He was heartbroken over the way His creation had turned out. His plan was perfection – but we abused the free will that was intended to be part of that perfection. He created us to be in His image. He'd never done that before in creation. Can you image watching something that you love so much slowly destroy itself?

As painful as the Great Flood and the events of Good Friday were for God the Father to watch, He allowed them to happen because He sees the big picture. The earth needed the cleansing of the flood and, even more importantly, the earth needed the cleansing of the cross. Jesus wasn't really forsaken, but He certainly expressed an emotion that we all experience at those times when we feel like we are alone in our suffering. God the Father willingly allowed Jesus to suffer and die on the cross – out of His great love for us all. As painful as it was for Him to watch, God the Father wanted the big picture of eternal life to include you and me!

You have a heavenly Father who hurts when you hurt. He is right there beside you, holding you in His arms during those moments when you are suffering and feeling alone. He sees the painful look in your eyes and He hears your tearful cries. And through the pain – and the triumph – of the cross, He has prepared a place for you in heaven. Jesus did it all for you.

Pray about It

Dear Father,

Thank You so much for sending Your Son Jesus to die on a cross for my sins – and for all the sins of the world! It is because of sin that we all must endure pain and inevitable heartache in this life; and yet I know that nothing compares to the heartache You must have felt when Your own beloved Son cried out to You on the cross. Father, bestow upon me Your comfort when I am hurting, or when someone in my family is suffering. In Jesus' name, Amen.

Talk about It

- Think of some of the greatest hardships you have faced in your life. Why do you think God allowed them to happen? Did these events ultimately bring you into a closer relationship with Him?

- In our times of suffering, what a difference it makes to know that God is right beside us, and He has a plan and a purpose for our situation. How does this knowledge help you to trust in God's plan for your life?

Live It Out

As a family, put together a special gift basket for an individual or a family that is grieving the loss of a loved one. Bake a batch of cookies and wrap them up in the basket. Have your children create a handmade card; younger children can draw the pictures, while older children can add a comforting Bible verse. You may want to tuck in a small devotional book into the basket as well. Deliver your gift basket in person, if possible.

Hurry!

But do not forget this one thing, dear friends: With the Lord a day is like a thousand years, and a thousand years are like a day. The Lord is not slow in keeping his promise, as some understand slowness. Instead he is patient with you, not wanting anyone to perish, but everyone to come to repentance. (2 Peter 3:8-9)

Life keeps us busy. We're all busy. Even with all the latest high-tech gadgets around us that promise to save us time, we're still too busy. Our schedules are packed from morning until night, and there's still not enough hours in the day for all of the things we want to get done. We are accustomed to everything being fast. We expect instant gratification. Speed and efficiency are highly valued in our society. Have you noticed that when you ask someone how they've been, one of the most common responses is: "Busy!"?

Unfortunately, one of the most common words I find myself saying to my girls is "Hurry!" I tell them to hurry when we're trying to get out the door for school, when we're getting out of the car at our destination, and even when they are getting ready for bed at night. It's always "hurry-hurry-hurry." Of course, I justify it by telling myself that I'm teaching them to be prompt and on time. It's a part of learning how to be a responsible person, right?

Finally, one afternoon, as I was rushing the girls out the door once again, Maile turned to me and asked, "Daddy, how come we *always* gotta hurry?"

To this day, I still haven't answered her question. Sure, I could have given her the standard answer: "We don't want to be late." But I know she was asking something deeper. My heart sank when she asked that question. I don't want to be known as the Daddy who's always in a hurry.

· · · · ·

The day between Good Friday – when Jesus was crucified – and Easter Sunday – when Jesus rose from the dead – is traditionally called "Holy Saturday." It's really a day of nothing. In fact, Jerry Seinfeld would have loved it! It's the one day out of year when the Sacrament of the Altar is not to be administered. It's a day when we are to live as if Christ was still dead. It is supposed to help us get inside the mind of a first century follower of Jesus. They saw Him die, but they weren't sure what was going to happen next.

Jesus didn't rise from the dead immediately after he died. He remained dead for three days. He didn't "hurry" back. He came back at the appropriate time. God's timing can't be rushed.

Throughout the Bible, we see examples of God taking His time. He could have easily created the entire universe in one quick moment, but He took His time and crafted the world over six days instead (Genesis 1). Jesus could have raised Lazarus immediately after he died, but He chose to wait until Lazarus had been in the grave for four days, even to the point where "**he stinketh**." (The King James version of this story tells it best; John 11:39.) Jesus didn't even start His own ministry until he was 30 years old. Why didn't He start much younger? Remember that in His day, someone was considered an adult at the age of 13. Jesus would have been considered fairly old to start a new profession at age 30. In today's culture of doing everything fast and expecting instant results, we don't always understand the wisdom of God's timing.

Even now, Jesus has told us that He's coming back again – but He's not hurrying. He's waiting. He came into the world the first time in the **"fullness of time"** (cf. Galatians 4:4), and He'll come back when the time is right. Remember, the disciples fully expected that Jesus would return in *their* lifetime! But Jesus is waiting. Why? The Scriptures are clear; the news of Jesus must reach the furthest corners of the earth (cf. Matthew 24:14). Everyone needs to have the opportunity to hear of the love and grace we have in Jesus. He doesn't want anyone to perish. He's not hurrying because of His great love for us all. Maybe, out of love, we should not hurry so much either.

Holy Saturday has taken on new meaning for me in my hurried, busy life. It reminds me that I don't need to hurry all the time. I don't need to brag about how busy I am to make myself feel more important. That Saturday of waiting makes the Sunday of resurrection so much sweeter!

Pray about It

Dear Jesus,

In the hurried pace of my life, I often let less important things take priority over my worship and relationship with You. Help me to follow Your example and slow down!

Please grant me time to enjoy the peacefulness that comes with a slower-paced lifestyle, and the opportunities that open up when I become more available to You and my family. I pray this in Your name, Amen.

Talk about It

- What simple, quiet blessings have you missed this week in your busy, day-to-day rush? How can you slow down more and savor these special moments and gifts?

- Reflect on Matthew 24:14. How are you living out this verse in your daily life? What are you doing to proclaim Christ's love to the furthest corners of the earth – or even to the furthest corner of your neighborhood?

Live It Out

How can waiting make things sweeter? Sometimes the anticipation makes things even better. Try this exercise in delayed gratification. Purchase a chocolate cake from a bakery. Bring it home and set it aside in the refrigerator with a note instructing your family not to touch it until three days from now. Everyone will look forward to it with great anticipation. Does that first bite taste even better after you've waited?

Hiding and Hunting

Because of the LORD's great love we are not consumed, for his compassions never fail. They are new every morning; great is your faithfulness. (Lamentations 3:22-23)

One of the perks of being the offspring of a church worker was that Maile and Leilani were able to help hide 5,000+ stuffed Easter eggs for our congregation's annual Easter Egg Hunt. Even though it was a lot of work, the girls really looked forward to it every year. From the moment they got up on the Saturday morning before Easter, they would ask me every five minutes, "Is it time yet? Is it time yet?" When it finally was time, it usually took about two hours to hide all of the eggs, and yet their enthusiasm was maintained.

One year, I asked Maile which activity she liked better – hiding the eggs or hunting for them. She quickly responded, "Hiding them!" Now, this answer surprised me, because this girl *loves* candy! She's got a sweet tooth like no one else. When it comes time for the egg hunt on Easter morning, she's out there running as fast as she can. When her basket gets full, she dumps the contents into her little wagon, and then runs back out there to gather another basketful of those treat-filled eggs.

"Hiding them? Really?" I asked. "Why's that?"

"Well, it's fun to see all the kids get so excited when they find their eggs. And all the eggs are full of such wonderful surprises! It's more fun to hide them."

Maile certainly knew the fun of finding those little treasures in the grass, and the sweet surprises that were waiting inside each one. It made her happy to know that other kids would have that same joyful experience of discovery.

. . . . .

Do you like surprises? I have to confess that I really don't. I prefer being in control and knowing exactly what I'm getting ahead of time. But having a childlike faith includes an appreciation for the fun of a surprise. We are reminded in Lamentations chapter 3 that God's mercies are new every morning. God's love is full of surprises! His Son Jesus was born in a lowly *manger*, of all places! Feeding 5,000+ people with five loaves of bread and two fish – who saw *that* coming? Death is an inevitable part of life – and we can accept it – but someone *rising from the dead*? How can that be?

Sometimes God's goodness may not be so obvious to us; maybe we need to do a little "hunting" to see it. But it's always a pleasant surprise when we catch God at work in our lives.

I love the fact that Maile prefers hiding the surprises for others more than receiving them herself. She understands that it's about putting other people's needs first. It's about being selfless, instead of selfish. It's about sharing the joy of the surprise. It's one thing to be surprised by Jesus yourself, but it's a whole new reward to be used by God to surprise other people with His love! How can you surprise your family and friends? Be patient when there are disappointments (cf. Ephesians 4:2); be a peacemaker when there is discord (cf. James 3:18). How can you surprise your classmates or coworkers? Give a gentle answer when someone confronts you (cf. Proverbs 15:1). Look for opportunities to surprise the people who thought they knew all about you, and to share with them the bigger surprise of God's infinite mercies.

Pray about It

Dear Father,

Thank You for all of the wonderful blessings that You are always placing in my life. Parenthood itself is filled with so many surprises every day! I am constantly blessed by all the big and little surprises that You give to me through my children. Father, help me to find ways to surprise other people, too – especially by sharing the good news of Your amazing love. In Jesus' name I pray, Amen.

Talk about It

- When was the last time someone completely surprised you? When was the last time you surprised someone else? What makes a surprise so much more fun than always knowing what to expect ahead of time?

- Think of some of the ways that God's love surprises us anew each day. What person in your life could you surprise today with an illustration of God's uplifting love?

Live It Out

Gather your children together and play a game of hide-and-seek with a few of their favorite toys. Have the children cover their eyes while you hide the toys. Try to stash them in very unusual places where they wouldn't normally expect to find them. In addition to familiar toys, hide a brand-new one they've never seen before. When all the toys have been found, ask your children how surprised they were to find their toys in places where they least expected – and how exciting it was to find a completely new toy, too! Remind them that God's love is always new, and always full of surprises. Then, let the kids hide something for *you* to find!

Separation

For I am convinced that neither death nor life, neither angels nor demons, neither the present nor the future, nor any powers, neither height nor depth, nor anything else in all creation, will be able to separate us from the love of God that is in Christ Jesus our Lord. (Romans 8:38-39)

It was one of those days when my brain wasn't operating on all cylinders. Maile and I were driving around town running errands, and my mind was on a hundred other things that morning. In fact, it was everywhere except where it should have been. We stopped at the gas station to fill up, and I hopped out and started filling the car with gas, mentally running through the rest of my packed schedule for the day. After returning the gas pump to its holder, I turned back to the car to get inside – but the door refused to open. Suddenly I realized that all the doors were locked. I peered in and saw my keys still dangling from the ignition, where I had absent-mindedly left them. Ugh! How did I do *that*? And suddenly I glance in the backseat at Maile, who is strapped securely into her car seat, and I realize the bigger problem is not me being locked out of the car, but my child being locked inside it. So I do what any sensible husband would do in this situation – I call my wife and ask her to come down and meet me with a spare key. But she doesn't pick up the call. I leave as calm a voicemail as I can muster, while still urging her to hurry down as quickly as she possibly can to help us. Then it dawns on me that it might be quite a while before she even hears the message. Yikes!

I know it's a long shot, but I calmly ask Maile if she can wiggle and squeeze out of her car seat by herself. She tries, but she can't do it. Then I ask her to stretch her arm over as far as she can, hoping she can somehow unlock the door. But again, she can't. I was trying to act casual about it, hoping she wouldn't sense my panic. But suddenly she put two and two together and realized that Daddy is locked out of the car and she is separated from him. She starts to cry – brave tears at first, and then increasingly more frightened tears. She continues to struggle, trying to wiggle out of her car seat, and reaching in vain for the lock on the door. She's trying so hard that I can hear the "gnashing of teeth" from outside of the vehicle. My eyes start to tear up, watching my baby scared and reaching her arms out to me. I don't want her to think I've abandoned her, so I keep talking to her in loving and encouraging ways. But I can't touch her. I can't hold her and console her. The separation is suddenly unbearable for both of us. Her eyes plead for me to rescue her, as the tears spill down her little cheeks. It absolutely breaks my heart.

Finally, Mommy arrives at the gas station with the keys, and in a flash the door is open. I rush into the car, unbuckle the car seat, pull her out, and hold her tightly in my arms. Through her sobbing tears, she manages to say, "Thanks, Daddy, for saving me!"

(It probably should have been "Thanks, Mommy, for saving me!" – but who's keeping score?)

· · · · ·

A Biblical understanding of hell is separation from God – and all that God is: e.g., love, peace, mercy, justice (cf. Luke 16:19-26). In Romans 8 we are told, twice, that nothing can separate us from the love of God that is in Christ Jesus. God's love will always be there. But because of our sin, we sometimes do things that distance ourselves from Him. When we feel distant – when we are in those weeping and gnashing moments – we should cling all the more firmly to the promise that nothing can separate us from Jesus' love for us. The world will try its best to divide us from our Father. It will lie, deceive, and distract us. Satan would love nothing more than to have us believe that we are "locked out" of God's love and eternal salvation. But nothing can separate us. No matter what difficulties we face today, our Father is there waiting – ready to hold us tightly. Thank you, Lord, for such a wonderful and faithful promise!

Pray about It

Dear Father,

There is nothing like being in Your presence! Thank You for sacrificing Your Son Jesus to save me from being eternally separated from You. I am so thankful that I will always be with You, and that no matter what hardships and pain I may endure on this earth, nothing can ever separate me from Your love. Please continue to remind me every day that I am forever Yours! I pray these things in Jesus' name, Amen.

Talk about It

- Re-read Romans 8:38-39. Why do you think Paul made a point of listing these ten different things that he is convinced will not separate us from Jesus? Does this help us to better understand his point?

- Do you find that you feel distant and isolated from God when you rebel against Him with sinful thoughts, words or actions? Likewise, when you confess your sins to God, do you feel closer to Him again?

Live It Out

How can God use you to "save the day" for someone this week? Ask Him to show you someone who needs a reminder that God is always with them. Pray for opportunities to reach out to this person with a kind smile and a helping hand. Be open to what God may ask of you. You may be surprised how powerfully He uses you!

Carry Me

Sing the praises of the LORD, enthroned in Zion;
  proclaim among the nations what he has done.
For he who avenges blood remembers;
  he does not ignore the cries of the afflicted.
LORD, see how my enemies persecute me!
  Have mercy and lift me up from the gates of death,
that I may declare your praises
  in the gates of Daughter Zion,
  and there rejoice in your salvation. (Psalm 9:11-14)

When my daughters were younger, one of the most frequent requests I heard from them would have to be, "Carry me Daddy!" It didn't seem to matter where we were, or what we were doing. They wanted to be carried everywhere: at church, in the store, while walking to school, coming back from the playground, walking around Disneyland, when it was time for bed, etc. I have to admit that I loved carrying them. I much preferred to have them in my arms than in a stroller – even if we had to walk long distances. It was our cuddle-time together. It wasn't always easy to lug them along in the summer heat, but I still loved every minute of it. That's what Daddies are for, after all. We carry things.

By the time the girls reached the ages of 5 and 7, I noticed that they weren't asking me to carry them much at all anymore. It's funny – I had always assumed I would rejoice when they became more independent and stopped asking me to carry them, because there were times when they asked for it a lot! But now I confess that I miss it. It was nice to be needed in that way.

And nowadays, we have the opposite situation. When I pick them up to get out of the car or to get in and out of the grocery cart, I'll hold them in my arms... and in a matter of seconds they squirm and ask, "Daddy, can you put me down, please?"

And I do... but I secretly wish I could still hold them.

· · · · ·

The author of Psalm 9 is reaching out to God for mercy and protection as his enemies are surrounding him. What words does he use to ask for God's help? "**LIFT ME UP**." When we are scared, tired, and hurting, our heavenly Father shows us His mercy by picking us up and carrying us. It's all part of that right relationship. He longs to lift us up out of our painful situations, to cradle us and carry us. It's all part of His plan for us. God wants us to depend on Him and to rest in His arms for comfort, safety, and security.

When was the last time you let God carry you through your day? Do you try to walk through life on your own, only reaching up your arms to be lifted when you are utterly exhausted and defeated, unable to walk another step? We humans have a tendency to believe that God wants us to be independent and do as much as possible ourselves. Trite, well-meaning sayings like, "Do your best, and God will do the rest" give us a false idea of what God wants our relationship with Him to be like. Or perhaps we think that mature Christians don't need to be carried at all. That's simply not true! We are never too big to be lifted up into our Father's embrace! We need to be carried by our Father, not only when the sin and darkness of this world surround us and we are too weak to walk on our own, but even when we believe we are strong and think we don't need it. So often He looks down at our stubborn independent streak, wishing we would just reach up our arms and let Him hold us tenderly.

May this be your prayer today and always: "Lord, lift me up!"

Pray about It

Dear Father,

Help me to remember that You are always willing to lift me into Your arms. Your arms are solid and mighty, safe and secure, and can hold me up all of my life. Make me like a child again, wanting nothing more than to be carried and cradled by You. For in Your arms, I am always protected and loved. In Jesus' name I pray, Amen.

Talk about It

• Do you agree with the adage, "Do your best, and God will do the rest?" How might living by this motto prevent us from reaching out to God until we are already weary and suffering?

• At which time in our lives do you think we tend to lean on God the most – when we are spiritually young in our faith, or when we are more mature?

Live It Out

Think of times when someone came forth and helped "carry" you at a time in your life when you really needed an extra hand. As a family, brainstorm some different ways you can help "carry" someone else this week. Does a friend or neighbor need help emotionally, spiritually, physically, financially? Can you babysit for someone who can't afford a sitter? Maybe you can lend a sympathetic ear, or give someone a ride to a doctor's appointment. God can use you to lift someone up who really needs it!

Career Day

And Jesus grew in wisdom and stature, and in favor with God and man. (Luke 2:52)

When Maile was in kindergarten, her school held a "Career Day," an event where the students were supposed to dress up according to the job they would like to have when they grow up. Maile spent weeks ahead of time trying to decide what she wanted to be. She agonized over the decision as if this was her one shot to pick what she was going to be for the rest of her life! I've seen college students devote less time to picking their majors!

The first choice Maile came up with for Career Day was to become the character Gabriella from *High School Musical*. However, her mother wisely advised her to consider another position that provided more employment opportunities. Maile had always talked about becoming a veterinarian some day, but for some reason she didn't think it would be fun to dress up like one. Finally, at the last minute, she decided to dress up just like her kindergarten teacher. Such a wonderful role model! May we never forget the power of a good teacher!

· · · · ·

What do we want our kids to be? All parents have some dream or vision of what they want for their children's future. I imagine that even Mary and Joseph had aspirations for their son, Jesus, as He was growing up. Scripture doesn't really tell us much about Jesus' childhood, but a little glimpse into His adolescence is given to us in Luke 2:52 where it says, **"as Jesus grew up, he increased in wisdom and in favor with God and people.**" (Today's NIV translation)

At first glance, you might think that this simple sentence doesn't tell us much detail about Jesus. But actually, it tells us a lot. Think about the four areas of growth mentioned here:

1. *"Jesus grew up."* He grew physically into a man.

2. *"He increased in wisdom."* He became more knowledge-able and intellectual.

3. *"(He grew) in favor with God."* Jesus became more spiritually mature, continually growing closer to His heavenly Father.

4. *"(He grew in favor) with people."* Jesus became more socially adept. He learned how to listen, to share, to en-courage, and to lead. He learned what it meant to be a friend.

   As you can see, these are four major areas of development. I want my daughters to grow in all these important ways as well. Development in these four areas will give them a good, well-rounded foundation, which will strengthen them and guide them in whatever career they may choose someday.

Close your eyes and imagine your child as an adult. What is his or her vocation? Do you envision a doctor? A salesman? An engineer? An actress? A pastor, DCE, or teacher? Some kids seem to know even at an early age exactly what they want to do, and as adults they settle quickly into a career that gives them a lifetime of satisfaction. Others try on a few different hats along the way before they find the best career choice. We may not even be able to venture a guess right now as to what jobs our children will ultimately hold. But God already knows. Isn't it amazing to realize that their future is already in God's hands? As parents who are raising our children to become faithful Christians, Luke 2:52 gives us good direction for the journey, so that whatever vocation our sons and daughters someday choose, they will grow up to be powerful witnesses of God's love to all whose lives they touch.

Pray about It

Dear Father,

I pray that You will help us as parents to raise our children in the knowledge of Your saving love, and to teach them to follow You and walk in Your ways. Please be with our children as they grow physically, spiritually, socially, and intellectually. Guide them to make the best possible choices for a successful and happy future. In Jesus' name, Amen.

Talk about It

- How were you encouraged to develop in each of these areas (physically, spiritually, socially, and intellectually) when you were young? How did this encouragement influence your future career or vocation?

- Sometimes parents place a great deal of pressure on their children to choose the "right" career. Would you be likely to steer your children toward certain vocations and away from others? Why?

Live It Out

You don't have to wait for a designated "Teacher Appreciation Day" to express gratitude to a wonderful teacher! Help your child create a colorful, handmade thank you card for his or her teacher. Encourage him to write his own words inside the card, if he is old enough. Bring it to school this week with a pretty bouquet of flowers or a small gift. You may want to do something similar yourself – write a thank you letter to a teacher or mentor from your elementary or high school years who influenced you and made an impact on your life.

What Does Daddy Do?

When he had finished washing their feet, he put on his clothes and returned to his place. "Do you understand what I have done for you?" he asked them. "You call me 'Teacher' and 'Lord,' and rightly so, for that is what I am. Now that I, your Lord and Teacher, have washed your feet, you also should wash one another's feet. I have set you an example that you should do as I have done for you. Very truly I tell you, no servant is greater than his master, nor is a messenger greater than the one who sent him. Now that you know these things, you will be blessed if you do them."
(John 13:12-17)

When Maile was three years old, the wonderful teachers at her preschool compiled a scrapbook of each child's experiences throughout the school year. Maile's book was filled with various pictures, drawings, and other artwork, some homework pages, and, particularly intriguing, her answers to some of the questions of life.

One of these questions was, "What does your daddy do for work?" Maile had replied, "Well, my daddy's gone a lot." (Ouch! There's nothing like hearing that come out of the mouth of your little girl – not exactly the memory of Daddy I wanted to leave her!) But then she had added, "He gives money to people."

At first I wondered where she got that. I really don't have much of my own money, let alone much to give away. But as I thought about it more, I realized that she had noticed the times when I would announce the collection of the offering at church, and when I would organize special fund-raisers for the support of missionaries, mission teams, or local/global causes.

I think what Maile had meant to convey was that her daddy helps people. Now, *that* is a legacy that I want to pass down to my children. As a family, we try to help whomever we can, whenever we can. While we few can't help everyone, we assist those God places into our lives, with the strength He provides.

Why? Because we know from Jesus' example that it's not about being served – it's about serving. Jesus sums this up best in Matthew 20:28 – **"the Son of Man did not come to be served, but to serve, and to give his life as a ransom for many."** Yes, Jesus has established the ultimate example of service by giving His very life as a sacrifice for our sins.

Now that we have learned from Jesus' example, He promises to bless us spiritually if we do likewise (cf. John 13:17). Bettering other's lives betters our own life.

What do you do for work?

Pray about It

Dear Jesus,
    Please give me a servant's heart! I long to be like You. Instead of thinking merely about what others can do for me,

help me focus on how to serve the needs of those around me and bring Your love into their life through my words and deeds. Open my eyes and heart to see and understand whom You've placed in my life to reach out and serve. May I humbly follow Your example of service, expecting nothing in return. In Your name I pray, Amen.

Talk about It

- Jesus wants us to show His love to others through the everyday moments of our lives, right where we happen to be. Whether you are a factory worker, a teacher, a farmer, or a stay-at-home parent, you have unique opportunities to reach out to others with the love of Christ. What are some ways you can share Him with others where you live and work?

- What are some of the spiritual legacies that you want to pass down to your children?

Live It Out

Jesus set an example of humble service for us to follow. Find a local charity, food bank, or nonprofit organization you would like to support, and volunteer for the day. Your church can suggest some worthy organizations that would be grateful for the gift of your time. If possible, plan to volunteer as a family. At the end of the day, talk about how it felt to help others and which aspects of serving were the most rewarding for each family member.

154

Blessing

When he had led them out to the vicinity of Bethany, he lifted up his hands and blessed them. While he was blessing them, he left them and was taken up into heaven. Then they worshiped him and returned to Jerusalem with great joy. And they stayed continually at the temple, praising God. (Luke 24:50-53)

"Daddy, I want to be you," Leilani said to me one afternoon, during one of those special daddy-daughter moments as we cuddled on the couch together.

"Really, honey?" I asked her, genuinely surprised by her remark. "That's kind of funny, because I just want you to be *you.* You're so smart and funny and beautiful."

She squeezed me tightly, basking in my praise. After a moment's pause, she looked up at me with her big brown eyes and said, "What else, Daddy?"

I smiled down at her. "Well, let's see. There are so many things that make you special. You're so good at praying. I love how you talk to Jesus. You make my faith stronger when you pray with me. And you're a great artist! I'm so proud of all your pictures. Each one is as lovely as you are. And you have such a beautiful singing voice. You sound like an angel from heaven."

"Ohhhh," Leilani smiled to herself. "What else, Daddy?"

"Well, you are such a good friend. I like the way you always have something nice to say to everyone. You care about other people's feelings. And you are a great little sister to Maile. She is so lucky to have a sister like you!"

Leilani grinned, and then nudged me to continue. "What else?"

We went back and forth for twenty minutes. I kept affirming her, reminding her of her many special talents and gifts, and all the things about her that make her unique and wonderful. She loved every second of it.

· · · · ·

We all need to be blessed and affirmed. It makes us feel appreciated, valued, and important, especially when it comes from someone we love. Unfortunately, we live in a world where positive affirmation is not always the norm. Sometimes it seems like everyone is much more focused on what we do wrong than what we do right. Criticism and judgment seem to be the themes of the day. Perhaps we are guilty of this mindset as well, even in our own families. Ask yourself these two questions: (1) When was the last time you scolded your child, or pointed out his or her faults or weaknesses? And (2) when was the last time you praised your child for something they did well, or for a quality they possess? For that matter, when was the last time you blessed your spouse with words of encouragement and affirmation? We want to think of ourselves as a supportive parent or a loving spouse, but if we could tape-record most of the words that come out of our mouths and hear ourselves, I think we would all be surprised how negative we can be – even toward the people we love the most.

Have you ever noticed how Jesus blessed His disciples in the Ascension account in Luke chapter 24? He raised His hands and blessed them, so they could see the nail scars in His hands and were reminded of the incredible sacrifice He had made for them. Then it says that **"while He was blessing them, He left them."** He was blessing, affirming, and showing them His incredible love for them, even as He ascended up into heaven. In fact, it never states that He ceased the blessing at any point in His ascension. That's because Jesus has never stopped blessing His followers! He's still bestowing His love upon us. He knows that we will have many troubles in this world (cf. John 16:33), and while we are here, we need to be continually blessed, affirmed, and reminded that we have incredible worth in Him.

We have been blessed for a reason – so that we, in turn, may be a blessing to others. Instead of being just one more critical, negative voice in the world, let's pass on the love and hope that Jesus has given us. Share an affirming word with someone who needs to hear it. Tell your spouse how wonderful he is at listening and how much you appreciate it. Praise your child for being patient and considerate to others on the playground. Compliment your coworker for her skills in the office, and let her know how much she is valued. Instead of noticing where others fall short, give them a positive word of appreciation and admiration for what they do well. How can you bless someone today?

Pray about It

Dear Father,
　　How amazing it is that You can use me to be a blessing to others! Keep me mindful to share words of affirmation, praise, and appreciation with others. Help me to see those who need to hear those words the most. You are truly the source of every single blessing in my life. May I be forever grateful of Your love and kindness! I pray these things in Jesus' name, Amen.

Talk about It

- How does the act of blessing and affirming others remind us of our precious worth in Christ?

- It's one thing to encourage people we love, but Jesus also calls us to love our enemies. It's not always easy to show kindness to someone who is mean or disagreeable. What "enemy" of yours – someone you really don't like – could you make a habit of intentionally giving joy and love to?

Live It Out

Have each member of your family write down the name of someone in their lives who could use their blessing and affirmation. Perhaps this list will include someone you work with, a neighbor, or an extended family member. Look for opportunities to encourage them this week. Even a simple "I appreciate you!" can mean a great deal to someone. Remember that blessings can come through our actions as well as our words. A small child can color a picture for a neighbor, or bring a flower to her preschool teacher.

Summer

162

The Hike

"Come, follow me," Jesus said, "and I will make you fishers of men." (Matthew 4:19, NIV 1984)

Leilani and I have always loved to go on hikes together. We love getting out into the woods, hills, and canyons to explore God's beautiful creation. Whenever we hit the trail, Leilani comes well-equipped for exploration and adventure. She puts on her pink baseball cap, straps her pink hydration bottle to her waist, and always wears her Camo Velcro® sneakers – which is very funny, because she also has a book at home called *Princesses Don't Wear Hiking Boots*. (And by now, I'm sure you've all figured out that she's a princess!)

When Leilani was younger, I used to carry her in a front pack or a backpack, and sometimes I would simply carry her in my arms. Now that she's older, she proudly tackles even the most challenging terrain on her own two feet. This has also been a way for her to gain some independence and push herself a little bit, as some of the trails are steep and require extra vigilance and care in going up and down the paths. Sometimes they are muddy or strewn with rocks, and then the path becomes even more intimidating.

I'll never forget one particular time when I brought Leilani along for an afternoon hike in the hills. Soon after we started along the trail, she stopped and stared quietly at the hills ahead, surveying the challenge before her. Then she looked at me and announced, "Daddy, I'm gonna need to hold your hand when we go up and down the mountains." (They were really just small hills, but when your legs are little, the hills can easily feel like mountains!)

I nodded understandingly. I knew how independent she liked to be on the trails, and that it was hard for her to admit that she might need a hand. "Okay, honey, you can hold my hand when we go up and down."

"Thank you, Daddy."

"But what about when it's flat land?"

Leilani smiled at me. "Oh, Daddy! I don't need to hold your hand when I'm following you!"

. . . . .

Life is quite a hike. It's filled with ups and downs, hills and valleys. Sometimes the path is flat and easy, and sometimes it's steep and winding. At times, when we are overwhelmed or tired, even the small hills can feel more like mountains to us. The ups and downs can be very scary. So many things are completely unpredictable and out of our control.

And yet, we are never left to struggle alone on the paths of life. The very first command Jesus gave His disciples was "**follow me**" (Matthew 4:19). Wherever He leads, that's where we go! Our first and greatest calling is simply to follow Him. What a comfort and assurance this is for us! We don't have to wonder how we'll ever climb those hills, or how we'll find our way back when we get lost. Jesus is there for us, with sure and solid footing, no matter what the terrain might be.

Thank you, Jesus, for being there with us along life's journey. Thank you for leading us, holding our hand, and for supporting and loving us along the way!

Pray about It

Dear Jesus,

My life is filled with hills that sometimes feel like mountains. I can become overwhelmed so easily as I look at the challenging paths that lie ahead. I am so thankful that I am not walking these trails alone. You know every step I take; You know the path ahead and the ultimate destination. And when the mountains do come, remind me that You are right by my side supporting me all the way to the top. In Your name I pray, Amen.

Talk about It

- If you were to draw a "trail map" of your life thus far, what would it look like? Would it be a fairly flat, easy path, or would there be plenty of difficult mountains to climb? Does the reassurance that Jesus is walking with you and holding your hand influence the way you look ahead to the rest of the journey?

- It makes sense that following should be easier for us than leading; and yet, all too often, we forge ahead stubbornly on our own path instead of following where God wants to lead us. Why do we often struggle with the idea of letting Him lead the way?

Live It Out

Plan a hike together as a family. You can choose a short path at a local park, or a more ambitious trail further away. Discuss what items you will need to bring for your comfort and safety – hats, drinking water, good footwear, first aid kit, etc. You may want to print out a trail map, if one is available; older children can be in charge of following your progress on the map. Plan a fun surprise (like a special snack) to share together when you reach the end of the trail to celebrate your accomplishment.

The Cricket

The LORD said, "Go out and stand on the mountain in the presence of the LORD, for the LORD is about to pass by." Then a great and powerful wind tore the mountains apart and shattered the rocks before the LORD, but the LORD was not in the wind. After the wind there was an earthquake, but the LORD was not in the earthquake. After the earthquake came a fire, but the LORD was not in the fire. And after the fire came a gentle whisper. (1 Kings 19:11-12)

Maile really loves animals, and wants to be a veterinarian when she grows up. I find this rather funny because I'm not much of an animal lover myself. I don't mind going to the zoo, but I really don't like the idea of animals jumping on me or being in my house. But I always try to be supportive of my girls and their love for all creatures great and small.

A few summers ago, on a trip to Arizona to visit my brother Nathan, we spent a few days at the Grand Canyon. Maile was able to see all kinds of wildlife. She was so excited to spot deer and elk, mules and horses, and even an eagle. What a great experience! My brother was even so wise as to set us up to "camp" – "Christy-style" – at one of the lovely hotel lodges! It was a weekend of family fun.

On the long drive home, Maile and I talked about all the wonderful animals out in God's beautiful creation. I asked her which animal at the Grand Canyon was her favorite. I imagined she would say it was the majestic eagle soaring across the sky, or the friendly burro she had been thrilled to pet. But without skipping a beat she replied: "The cricket!"

"The cricket?" I was shocked. "I never saw a cricket. When did you see a cricket?"

"I saw a cricket, Daddy!"

During all of our hiking and exploring, I had been so busy looking at the bigger scene, the grandeur all around us, while Maile had noticed the small stuff. Maybe kids tend to notice what's on the ground because they are closer to it. But I think it's more than that. Children are wide-eyed observers in a world that's still very new to them. They may not care as much for the dramatic scenery in front of them as they do for the fuzzy caterpillar crossing their path, or a pretty little rock that catches their eye.

· · · · ·

Childlike faith notices the small stuff – the little blessings that God gives us every day. These are the things that can be very easy for us as adults to overlook at times. It's much easier to focus on the bigger things. But like the small, still voice that spoke to Elijah in 1 Kings 19, God is in the small stuff. Yes, there are plenty of examples in the Bible where God is found in the bigger things – sometimes He talks through earth-quakes and fire and big bold leaders – but He still calls us to be like little children (cf. Matthew 18:3). He wants us to pay attention to the small stuff.

Albert Einstein said that we really only have two ways to look at the world. One way is to say that there are no such things as miracles, while the other is to say that everything is a miracle. Childlike faith sees the miracles in everything from the stars in the sky to a cricket. God created it all. It's all part of His plan. By His direction, all of the little details come together in perfect harmony.

Small stuff can make a big difference. A little kindness goes a long way. A little extra time can mean the world to someone. A smile can change someone's day! We're often told that we shouldn't sweat the "small stuff," but sometimes it's when we slow down long enough to catch a breath on our earthly journey that we are best able to see the small details of God's creation, to hear the subtle tones of God's message for us, and to understand how even we play a role in God's ultimate plan.

Pray about It

Dear Father,

Your creation is vast and beautiful, and there is more to see and appreciate than we could ever notice in a lifetime. Still, I pray that You will help me to find beauty and significance in the things that I might often overlook. Help me to slow down and notice all the little things that You have given me to enjoy. Please expand my vision so that I may see Your glory in the most unlikely of places. Thank You for all You have given to us. In Jesus' name, Amen.

Talk about It

- Sometimes in our busy lives, we may fail to notice God's small miracles all around us: a butterfly fluttering past our window, a child's sweet smile, the soft feel of a dog's fur, a flower blooming in our yard. How can you slow down and become more observant of God's presence and purpose in the small, seemingly insignificant things?

• What small, "cricket-like" efforts can you make today to enrich and bless the lives of those around you?

Live It Out

As a family, go for a walk in an area that's very familiar to you – your own street, your favorite park, maybe even your own backyard. Try to look carefully and attentively at the details of your surroundings, and see how many brand-new things you can find in this familiar area. Have each person point out something they've never taken the time to notice before. You may even want to take turns wearing a blindfold, and focusing on observing new things through your other senses.

The Road Trip

So the LORD gave Israel all the land he had sworn to give their ancestors, and they took possession of it and settled there. The LORD gave them rest on every side, just as he had sworn to their ancestors. Not one of their enemies withstood them; the LORD gave all their enemies into their hands. Not one of all the LORD's good promises to Israel failed; every one was fulfilled. (Joshua 21:43-45)

In the summer of 2010, we took the longest road trip of our young family's history. With an excited five-year-old and seven-year-old, we traveled 1,362 miles (but who's counting?) from Austin, Texas, all the way to Orange, California, and then another 1,362 miles back again. Christy and I were a little nervous about the journey. We had never traveled more than 300 miles in one shot with the girls in tow. Leilani had suffered from bouts of motion sickness during long car rides in the past. So we really had no idea what to expect.

I'm happy to announce that the trip went very well. The girls got along peacefully most of the time. We did have to enforce some "quiet time-out," but all and all, they were very good. We played all kinds of car games to pass the time. We even wrote some new silly songs. But there was one painful incident that still upsets me whenever I think about it.

Leilani tends to be a little picky when it comes to eating out in restaurants. During our trip, she was going through a phase when she really loved Subway. Now, ironically, this was after several years of crying miserably whenever we went to a Subway – but for now, it had become her favorite place to eat.

During the long days on the road, the girls took turns choosing where we stopped to eat for each meal. One morning, knowing it was her turn to choose the venue for lunch, Leilani made sure to request Subway. These days, it seems like there are almost as many Subway restaurants dotting the landscape as McDonald's. They are everywhere... usually... except when you really need one.

I promised Leilani we would find a Subway for lunch. At 10 a.m. she saw the familiar yellow sign by the side of the road and screamed: "DADDY! SUBWAY!"

"I know, honey, but it's not lunchtime yet." I reassured her that we would find another one when it was lunchtime.

Famous last words! You can probably guess what happened next. Around 11:30 a.m. we started keeping our eyes open for a Subway. We didn't see one. The noon hour came and went – and still no Subway. It was now 1:30 p.m. and everyone in the family was starving. Still, there wasn't a Subway in sight. As the long miles of Arizona desert stretched ahead of us, I knew we had better stop and eat as soon as possible, or there might be a mutiny in the minivan. The search for Subway would have to be abandoned.

"Okay girls," I announced, glancing back at their little faces in the driver's mirror. "It's now past lunchtime, and I know we are all really hungry. So the next restaurant we see, we're going to stop and get lunch." Within a few more miles, lo and behold – on the horizon came a Dairy Queen, and not a minute too soon for my growling stomach.

As I pulled into the parking lot, Leilani suddenly realized what was going on, and she screamed: "BUT DADDY, YOU *PROMISED*!"

Those words cut deep. I had broken a promise to my daughter. I have always preached the importance of keeping one's word and not breaking promises, and here I was breaking one myself. My heart sank, and as we climbed out of the car, I went over and hugged Leilani tightly. I apologized for breaking my promise, reminding her that I tried my best, but it was important for us to find something to eat. She was still upset for a while, but hungrily ate her Dairy Queen lunch. Ice cream usually has a way of making things a little bit better.

· · · · ·

We serve a God who never breaks His promises. His grace, mercy, and love never waiver. Joshua, the successor of Moses who led God's people of Israel into the Promised Land, declared: "**Not one of all the LORD's good promises to Israel failed; every one was fulfilled.**" (Joshua 21:45) Every single one! It's so hard for us to even imagine being able to keep all of the promises we make in our lives. Sometimes we make a casual promise to someone, and then we completely forget that we made it. Sometimes we decide that some of the promises we made in the past aren't really important anymore, and we choose to let them lapse. And sometimes, in spite of our very best efforts, circumstances outside of ourselves prevent us from being able to make good on our promises to others. We are sinful, and we live in a sinful world.

But God is perfectly faithful. He never breaks His promises – promises of unconditional love, forgiveness, hope, a meaningful life now, and ultimately eternal life with Him. Hold fast to these promises, for you can always count on them. Memorize them. Cling to them. And know that God will never break them!

By the way, when we got back on the road, sure enough – there was a Subway two more exits down the road! Keeping promises can be a challenge, but not for our heavenly Father.

Pray about It

Dear Father,
    Thank You for Your unfailing love! You are an amazing and reliable God, and I am constantly reminded of this by all of my daily blessings. You have done so much for me, even though I am completely undeserving. But still, You always keep Your promises to provide, protect, guide, and love me always! It is because of Your enduring goodness that I can faithfully await the day that I am called to heaven to spend eternity in Your presence! In Jesus' name, Amen.

Talk about It

- Sometimes, when painful things happen in our lives, we may wonder if God has broken His promises to us. *Has He abandoned me? Does He still love me? Will He really forgive such a terrible sin?* Share a time when you doubted the promises that God has made to you.

- Have you ever broken a promise to your child? Your spouse? Your best friend? What consequences did you pay for your broken promise? Do you think other people consider you to be a reliable person, or is this an area where you could improve?

Live It Out

Think of a promise that you made recently to someone in your family, but one that you haven't yet fulfilled. Maybe you promised to take the kids to the mall, the beach, or the amusement park "someday soon, when I have time." Or perhaps you promised your spouse that you would take care of a household project that's been sitting on your to-do list for a long time. Make a firm decision today that you will keep your promise, and set aside a specific day or time to fulfill it. By keeping your word, you will be sending a powerful message to your loved one that they are worth honoring.

176

Measuring Up

As Jesus started on his way, a man ran up to him and fell on his knees before him. "Good teacher," he asked, "what must I do to inherit eternal life?" "Why do you call me good?" Jesus answered. "No one is good – except God alone. You know the commandments: 'You shall not murder, you shall not commit adultery, you shall not steal, you shall not give false testimony, you shall not defraud, honor your father and mother.'" "Teacher," he declared, "all these I have kept since I was a boy." Jesus looked at him and loved him. "One thing you lack," he said. "Go, sell everything you have and give to the poor, and you will have treasure in heaven. Then come, follow me." At this the man's face fell. He went away sad, because he had great wealth. Jesus looked around and said to his disciples, "How hard it is for the rich to enter the kingdom of God!" (Mark 10:17-23)

Sometimes it's tough to be little. When you're four years old, it seems like the best things in life are out of your reach. This is especially true at amusement parks, where there's a certain height requirement to go on the most exciting rides – like the roller-coasters and all those other things that turn you upside down and can make you sick.

Leilani has always been small for her age. And when you live in Orange County, California, and Disneyland is practically in your backyard, height becomes a *very* important factor.

One summer day at Disneyland, Leilani was oh-so-close to finally meeting the magical 42-inch mark – and therefore being allowed to go on several of the rides she had been anticipating for a long time. We were so certain that she was finally tall enough this time, but alas, we were mistaken – she was *still* a bit too short. When Leilani heard that she was still measuring short of the mark, she sat down on a bench and cried miserably. Since we were moving to Texas soon, we knew that this would be our last trip to Disneyland for a while. My heart went out to her, and I decided to stuff the inside of her shoes with some padding to make her a little bit taller so she would meet the height requirement. It worked, and she was allowed to go on the Matterhorn, a ride she'd been waiting to go on her whole life. She loved it. And after that one, we got in line for Space Mountain since the height requirement was the same. While we waited in the long queue, I started telling Leilani how much she was going to enjoy the upcoming ride. Suddenly, Leilani started to cry.

"What's wrong, honey?" I said. "Don't be scared – it's going to be a great ride!"

"My feet hurt so bad, Daddy!"

Leilani reached down and tried to readjust the padding in her shoes. I could tell she was really uncomfortable.

"But honey, if you don't have all of that extra stuff in your shoes, you're not going to be tall enough to go on the ride."

Leilani was quiet for a minute, thinking about her choices. Then she looked up at me with a painful look and wailed:

"But Daddy! My feet hurt SO BAD!"

I picked her up and carried her out of the queue area. While Mommy and Maile stayed in line, Leilani and I sat down on a bench and took the padding out of her shoes. Now she wouldn't be able to go on the "tall rides," but her feet would feel much better for the rest of the day.

The more I started to think about it, the more I felt ashamed for teaching her that it was okay to cheat the system. I had always taught my girls the importance of being honest and obeying the rules – and now I had asked Leilani to do something that wasn't right. Of course, I thought I had justification for doing it. But in the end, it was still wrong.

Measuring up is hard to do. Leilani had cried when she was too short for the rides and didn't measure up – and then she cried even more when we tried to "fake" her measurement. And what's more, in my own way, I had failed to measure up as well.

. . . . . .

In Mark chapter 10, Jesus encounters a young man who is striving to measure up. He claims to have kept all of the commandments. Had he? We can safely assume that he hadn't because no one except Jesus has ever kept the Law perfectly. But Jesus never calls him a liar. This young man seems to be earnestly seeking to inherit eternal life. Notice it says in verse 21 that when Jesus looked at him, He "*loved him*." It really seems like this man was sincere in his efforts to please God, and he really wanted to know how to measure up.

Jesus looks straight into the man's heart and knows what is still holding him back. Jesus tells him to sell everything he owns, to give to the poor, "**and you will have treasure in heaven**" (verse 21). But because he was a very rich man, he just couldn't do it. He was so close – but he couldn't bring himself to sacrifice what was truly important to him. He, too, could not measure up.

Jesus knew from the beginning that this guy didn't measure up. But Jesus looked at him and loved him anyway. He looks at us with that same love, even though none of us can measure up either. ALL have sinned and fallen short of the dream that God has for us (cf. Romans 3:23). But Jesus loves us anyway. He doesn't want us to continue sinning, of course, but He forgives us where we have fallen short. He loves us deeply despite our sin. Jesus loves us to the full measure!

Pray about It

Dear Jesus,
    You are the ultimate role model for the world, and as Your follower, I strive to follow You and live up to the standards and values that You have set for us. But I was born a sinner, and as a result, I will never be able to fully measure up. Thank You for Your unconditional love, Lord! Thank You for looking at me and loving me, even though I often fall short. I am so grateful for the sacrifice You made for me so that I am restored and given new life in You. In Your holy name I pray, Amen.

Talk about It

- Jesus can look into the depths of our heart and know what is holding us back. What are some specific things that are holding you back from measuring up to what God expects from You?

- We often believe that we have good reasons for our sinful actions, and we tend to justify them to ourselves and others. Do you think God accepts our reasons for sin? If not, then why do *we*?

Live It Out

For generations, parents have been marking their children's heights on the inside of closet doors. Chances are good that your parents kept a similar chart for you when you were little. Are you carrying on this tradition with your own family? Children delight in watching their growth progress marked in such a visual way. Choose a spot in your home to record these milestones for each child, along with their name, height and date. Do this at least once a year to let them see how they "measure up."

The Soak Zone

As they traveled along the road, they came to some water and the eunuch said, "Look, here is water. What can stand in the way of my being baptized?" (Acts 8:36)

One summer, on a trip to Sea World in San Diego, Maile and Leilani were excitedly looking forward to seeing the Shamu Show. As we entered the world-famous Shamu Stadium, Maile asked me if we could sit in one of the first 35 rows of seats, affectionately known as the "Soak Zone." Now, back when I was a kid, I remember it was called the "Splash Zone." But over the years this area of seats has moved far beyond "splash" and evolved into "soak." Now, if it had been noontime on a miserably hot day, the decision whether or not to sit in the Soak Zone might have been easier. But evening was quickly approaching. As the sun was starting to set, the breeze blowing inland from the ocean brought a chill that was already creeping up on us. So like any good father would do, I responded to Maile's seating request with the reply, "Honey, ask your mother."

Much to my surprise, my wife – the same person who says she's freezing in 80 degree weather – said, "Sure, you guys can sit down there!" Note the terminology here: "*you guys* can sit down there." There was no way that *she* was going to sit down there! I honestly thought there was no way that Mommy would let us sit in the Soak Zone, but boy, was I wrong!

So, after my "Let's Ask Mommy" trick backfired, I looked Maile squarely in her big, beautiful blue eyes and said, "Honey, we'll sit wherever you want." Leilani decided that she'd rather sit with Mommy (ah, the wisdom of a three-year-old!). So while Leilani and Mommy climbed the stairs into the safe, dry, non-soak zone, Maile and I walked down – and down – and down, finally stopping at the 7th row from the very front, which was eye level to the massive tank of the beloved Killer Whale.

Maile was so excited! She couldn't wait for the show to start, and asked me every 30 seconds how much longer it would be. But when the Shamu Show finally started, her excitement soon waned – not because it wasn't a good show, but because she wasn't getting wet. Like a player on an opposing sports team, she started taunting Shamu. With every jump, flip, and splash, she shouted, "You didn't get me!" She even threw in an occasional "Ha, Ha!" Now, as a fairly educated adult, I know that whales have supersonic hearing, and one does not want to taunt a creature of that size – especially not one known as a "killer" whale! But without my high school biology classes to instill fear in her, Maile taunted away.

Finally, it happened. I'm not sure if Shamu just got sick of hearing insults from a 25 pound little girl or what, but he got us! And boy, did he get us good. "Soak Zone" was a drastic understatement that day. As I wiped the cold, fishy-smelling salt water from my eyes, I wondered if the rogue wave had completely washed my little girl away. Prepared to jump into the tank to save her, I looked over and saw Maile still sitting beside me, with the biggest, most beautiful smile on her face! She started doing the "Shamu Dance," more excited, energized, and captivated than she had been all day.

It then hit me. This experience wasn't about the water. It wasn't about getting wet, or even *soaked* for that matter. It was about an encounter – a *personal* connection – with that friendly killer whale, Shamu. He was the largest and most incredible animal Maile had ever seen. You just don't get to experience Shamu in quite the same way in the safe, dry, non-soak zone. And my little girl knew this. Maile was "blessed" by Shamu's splash in a way she'll never forget.

. . . . .

That's like Holy Baptism. It's not about the water. It's not about the amount, temperature, location, or "holiness" of the water. The water isn't special in and of itself. It's about an encounter – a connecting for all eternity with Jesus. Baptism is a cleansing – not through water, like a good shower – but a cleansing through the powerful, life-changing Word of God. It's the experiencing of forgiveness, and the promise of life everlasting. And it's the reminder that God desires the whole world to come to Him through the continually flowing waters of baptism.

Are you sitting in life's "Soak Zone?" Jesus tells us in Matthew 25:40, "**whatever you did for one of the least of these brothers and sisters of mine, you did for me.**" You encounter Jesus every day in the people around you. Are you seeing Jesus and connecting with Him through your inter-actions with other people – the waitress at your favorite restaurant? The barista at Starbucks? The parents of your four-year-old's friends? How can you see Jesus? And how can you BE like Jesus?

You don't experience Jesus the same way in the safe, dry, non-soak-zone. Sitting in the soak zone will get you wet –

and maybe a little smelly – but what a rush! So jump on in. The water's fine!

Pray about It

Dear Jesus,

So often I allow my own busyness to get in the way of my relationship with You. I may forget to pray, or I may let my mind wander during the sermon at church. I miss out on so many moments when I could be connecting with You. Jesus, I pray that I can let go of the daily things that get in my way, so that I can pour myself out to You and be "soaked" by Your love and Your words! In Your name I pray, Amen.

Talk about It

- What is it that makes encountering Jesus through the means of baptism so special and intimate? What does baptism mean to you?

- Often we experience a deep sense of God's presence in the times when we are closest to life's "soak zone." Think of a recent experience when this happened to you. Would you have grown as much in your faith if you had remained in the dry, safe zone?

Live It Out

Find a way to encounter Jesus in your community through helping those in need. Consider volunteering with your entire family at a local soup kitchen or food pantry. Try to find something even the youngest members of your family can do.

Eye on the Ball

And let us run with perseverance the race marked out for us. Let us fix our eyes on Jesus, the author and perfecter of our faith. (Hebrews 12:1-2)

Recently, I've been playing a lot of baseball in the backyard with my two daughters. After every pitch I make, I find myself saying, "Keep your eye on the ball." It's an involuntary reflex; I can't help it. It just comes out. I've been tempted to say, "There's no crying in baseball!" like Tom Hanks's character in *A League of Their Own*, but so far I've been able to restrain myself.

My dad always told me to keep my eye on the ball when we would play ball in the backyard. I'm sure his dad told him the same thing, and so on. In order to hit the ball, you can't lose focus. Staying focused means eliminating distractions, tuning out what's unimportant, and concentrating completely on the task at hand. But when you're four years old, it can be extremely difficult to eliminate distractions – after all, your whole life is one big distraction!

· · · · ·

The author of the book of Hebrews says: "**Let us fix our eyes on Jesus, the author and perfecter of our faith.**" (Hebrews 12:2) In other words, we need to keep our eye on the ball. We need to keep our hearts and minds centered on Christ, so we can live our lives for Him. And what's even better, we can also point the way for others. For many of us, the idea of sharing our faith with our friends and neighbors seems scary and overwhelming. We worry about what we should say, when we should say it, and how they might respond to us. We become so distracted by the "what ifs" that we forget to focus on the most important thing – Jesus! We become distracted and take our eyes off the ball. We swing and miss – or even more sadly, we may not swing at all.

The next time you have an opportunity to share your faith with others, try to keep your focus on what is really at the heart of it all. Simply talk to people about Jesus, your friend and brother – just as naturally and comfortably as you would talk about any of the important people in your life. Keep your focus on Jesus, and don't allow the distractions, fears, and doubts of the world to throw you off your game.

Leilani is starting to learn what it means to stay focused. The other day, our family decided to play an impromptu game of baseball at the park. I pitched the ball to Mommy, who swung wildly and missed. Little sweet Leilani yelled, "Mommy! Keep your eye on the ball!" (That's my girl!)

Pray about It

Dear Jesus,

Please help me to keep my eyes fixed on You. Help me to ignore the doubts and "what ifs" that haunt my thoughts, and remove the distractions that come with living life here on earth. I know that I need to keep my focus on You, so that I will be able to readily point other people to You as well. In Your holy name I pray, Amen.

Talk about It

- Reread Hebrews 12:1-2. What does it mean, in your day-to-day life, to "Fix your eyes on Jesus?"

- When have you found that it's most challenging to keep your eyes on Jesus – during the stressful, difficult times or during the easier, smoother periods of your life? Why?

Live It Out

Think of someone in your circle of friends, relatives, or co-workers who is struggling through a hard time right now and who could really use some spiritual encouragement to fix their eyes on Jesus. Perhaps you can invite them to church or a Bible study class. Offer to pray *with* them, not merely for them. Share a section or verse of Scripture that you have found particularly meaningful in times of discouragement.

Whom Do We Cheer For?

Finally, brothers and sisters, whatever is true, whatever is noble, whatever is right, whatever is pure, whatever is lovely, whatever is admirable – if anything is excellent or praiseworthy – think about such things. Whatever you have learned or received or heard from me, or seen in me – put it into practice. And the God of peace will be with you. (Philippians 4:8-9)

Raising two little princesses can be quite a challenge, especially considering that Daddy is a diehard sports fanatic. After all, our interests don't seem to naturally overlap very much. My idea of a relaxing Saturday afternoon is to hang out on the living room couch and watch a baseball or college football game – while my girls would much rather dress up in full princess regalia (gowns and jewels) and watch a fairy-tale movie. They beg me to sit and watch with them, and often I do. I think I have now seen every princess movie ever released, several times over!

I've always longed to pass down my love and knowledge of sports to my girls, but it's not always easy. The only time they ever want to watch sports with me is when it's already well past their bedtime and they want to get away with staying up late. And of course I let them do it, because there's something special about having them curl up with Daddy on the couch watching sports together.

While my girls may not actually be sports fans, I'm still trying to teach them to "talk the talk." They know what a hat trick is, what "shoot the gap" means, and what happens when a power forward goes baseline. And perhaps most importantly, they know they should *always* cheer for the Dodgers, Lakers, and the Cleveland Browns. (Yes, the Browns! To make a long story short, my Dad is originally from Cleveland, and, yes it has been really hard over the years!)

Our move from California to Texas proved to be very confusing for Maile and Leilani with regard to sports teams. Apparently I had forgotten to explain that one's team loyalty sticks with you, even when you move halfway across the country. On a recent afternoon, my wife Christy and the girls went to a baseball game with some friends. The Texas Rangers were hosting the Anaheim Angels. I was out of town that day, so I was a bit surprised when I received a panicked phone call from Maile from the stadium, shortly before the game was scheduled to begin.

"Daddy!" she cried into the phone. "We don't know what to do!"

"What's wrong, honey?" I said reassuringly, as my mind raced through all the possible scenarios that could be wrong. They had a flat tire on the way to the game? Leilani had gotten separated from them in the crowds? Someone got sick from eating a chili dog?

Maile's confused and innocent response made me smile. "Daddy, who do we cheer for at this game? The Angels or the Rangers?"

Proud to hear that they were taking this so seriously, I responded as any Daddy who's a Dodgers fan would respond:

"Honey, we *never* cheer for the Angels!"

Even though my girls don't really like sports, they do love cheering for a team. There's something exciting about rooting and pulling for a team to win. When they do, you feel like a winner too. You feel encouraged and validated because you are supporting something positive and admirable. Everyone loves to win!

. . . . .

In Philippians 4:8, St. Paul encourages us to focus on things that are positive and pleasing to God. He writes, "**whatever is true, whatever is noble, whatever is right, whatever is pure, whatever is lovely, whatever is admirable—if anything is excellent or praiseworthy—think about such things.**" There is a cheering nature to this passage, isn't there? We are to root for and support the best things in life. There are a lot of "teams" out there in the world – influences, ideas, groups, and popular trends – that are all competing for our allegiance. Many of them are not worth cheering for, and some would even love to lead us far off course from what God wants us to do. We are constantly faced with choices in our lives: Which way should we go? Whom do we listen to? Whom do we support and cheer for? Paul reminds us here that we are to focus on the pure, lovely, admirable things that are from God, and we can find out what those things are by studying His Word.

We are expected not merely to think about such things, but to actively search out and find the true, noble, right, pure, lovely, admirable, excellent, and praiseworthy things that may not be easily seen at first glance. It's about finding the best in people, even when they seem grumpy or sour. It's about finding the lovely in the seemingly unlovely things of this world. It's about discovering how our omnipresent God is at work even in those events and situations that don't seem to have His fingerprints on them. Sometimes this is a challenge. But finding and pursuing what is praiseworthy will help keep us focused on Jesus, and enable us to lead other people toward such things – and to show them the One who is responsible for it all.

In the course of your day today, how can you find more opportunities to "**think about such things**" (verse 8)? I'm cheering you on!

Pray about It

Dear Jesus,
    I pray that You will fill my heart and mind with those things that are true, noble, right, pure, lovely, admirable, excellent, and praiseworthy! The world makes it so easy to be lured over to the opposing team. Help me to focus on You, Jesus, so that I am always cheering for the right team. I pray, too, that You will use me to show others the path to eternal life and salvation. I pray this in Your holy name, Amen.

Talk about It

• Take a couple minutes and ask yourself, "What have I been cheering for in my life lately? Are these things noble, pure, or lovely?"

• Sometimes, without even realizing it, we let cynicism and negativity creep into our thoughts and words – especially within our own family. How can you actively seek out the good and admirable things in others, while focusing less on their flaws and mistakes?

Live It Out

Take your child to the park, pool, or playground. Assist and encourage them as they try out a new sport or master a particular skill: climbing the monkey bars, swimming across the pool, riding a bicycle, throwing and catching a ball. Be your child's greatest cheerleader! Affirm them every step of the way.

Lost!

Then Jesus told them this parable: "Suppose one of you has a hundred sheep and loses one of them. Doesn't he leave the ninety-nine in the open country and go after the lost sheep until he finds it? And when he finds it, he joyfully puts it on his shoulders and goes home. Then he calls his friends and neighbors together and says, 'Rejoice with me; I have found my lost sheep.' I tell you that in the same way there will be more rejoicing in heaven over one sinner who repents than over ninety-nine righteous persons who do not need to repent." (Luke 15:3-7)

One Saturday afternoon, when Maile was five years old and Leilani was three, I took the girls to a matinee. My brother was visiting and had come along with us to the theater. The girls had been looking forward to this movie for weeks; it promised to be a fun, animated action film.

However, the real action of the day didn't come from the silver screen, but from what happened when Leilani and I were returning to our seats following the second bathroom trip. This was one of those movie theaters with only one entrance/exit in and out, but two long aisles. Leilani was leading the way back into the theater, so while she headed straight to her seat, I thought I would walk under the stadium seating to the far aisle to get to my seat.

When I got to our row, I quickly noticed that Leilani was not in her seat. Hmm. Where was she? Looking around, I wondered if she had accidentally sat down in another row, thinking it was ours. The theater was fairly dark. I started walking back down the aisle to find her. The next thing I heard was a familiar, high-pitched scream that pierced me right to the soul. I started running toward the wretched wailing and found Leilani standing by the entrance, crying uncontrollably. "Daddy!" she screamed, throwing her arms around me and clutching me frantically, "I was LOST!"

Now before you nominate me for the "Worst Father of the Year Award," you should know that she was only "lost" for a total of seven seconds. But when you're three years old, seven seconds seems like a really long time! So Leilani and I sat on the floor together, just holding each other for a few minutes. The "lost" was found, and we eventually rejoiced with an Icee® and a bucket of popcorn!

· · · · ·

Among the many parables that Jesus taught, He gave three examples that relate to things being lost: the lost coin, the lost sheep, and the lost son (sometimes called the prodigal son) (Luke 15). While all three of the stories have a happy ending, it's interesting that Jesus chooses a coin, a sheep, and a son to illustrate His point. You see, the coin had no idea it was lost. It was just lost. And the owner rejoiced when it was found. The sheep unknowingly got lost. It just wandered off, as sheep often do. And the shepherd rejoiced when it was found. However, the third parable is a bit different. The son *chose* to get lost. The son knew the difference between right and wrong, but purposely chose the wrong path. He intentionally left. And still, when he realized his mistake and went back home, his father called for a huge party in his honor. There was great rejoicing and celebrating, because what was lost was now found!

These parables illustrate that nothing gives God greater joy than when the lost is found. Jesus summed up His whole reason for coming to earth in Luke 19:10 – **"For the Son of Man came to seek and to save the lost."** Note that Jesus isn't lost. People talk about "finding Jesus" in their lives, but they have it all backwards. We don't "find" Jesus. He finds *us*. We're the lost ones. Sometimes we don't know we're lost, like the coin. Sometimes we unintentionally wander off and get lost, like the sheep. And at other times, we flat out rebel and turn our backs on the Father. The story of the Prodigal Son is the story of you and me! But Jesus is always there to hold us, comfort us, and welcome us home. Remember that it doesn't matter how long we've been gone, or what has happened in the past. Jesus runs to meet us on the road, wraps His arms around us, and welcomes us home!

Pray about It

Dear Jesus,

I am comforted in knowing that You always know where I am, what decisions I will make, and where they will lead me. Even if those decisions should lead me astray, I know You are watching out for me – and that You will always come after me and lead me back into Your loving arms. Thank You for loving me so very much, my dear Shepherd! I pray this in Your name, Amen.

Talk about It

- Sometimes, like the prodigal son, we make the deliberate choice to get lost. We rebel and take the wrong path, believing that we know what's better for us than God does. How do we know for sure that He will always welcome us home when we return with a repentant heart?

- Few things in life can be as terrifying to a child as the experience of getting lost and separated from his or her parents. Think of a time when you were lost as a child, or your own child wandered away from you in a public place. What was your greatest fear? What was your greatest comfort?

Live It Out

Do you know someone in your life who is spiritually "lost?" How do you know? What are some ways you can be a witness to them of God's amazing grace and love? Start by showing them a glimpse of what they are missing. Make sure they know the true reason for the joy and hope you have in your life. Look for opportunities to introduce them to your church family. Invite them to join you in a community service event or activity sponsored by your church.

The Chair

Now faith is confidence in what we hope for and assurance about what we do not see. (Hebrews 11:1)

Leilani has always been my cuddler. When she was little, she would crawl into my lap and sit with me just about anywhere I happened to be. She would seize any opportunity she could find to nestle on my lap. She was so small and quiet that sometimes I would forget that she was there.

One evening, Leilani was sitting on my lap at a church event and, without warning, the chair that I was sitting on broke. There was a cracking sound and a crash. And before I could react, I was on the floor – still holding my sweet little Leilani in my arms. She was shaken up but fine. In fact, nothing was hurt but my pride. So I just pulled another chair over and sat down again.

After a few minutes, Leilani came back over and sat on my lap again. And wouldn't you know it, I heard the same cracking sound – and then the second chair broke! I couldn't believe it. Once again, I caught her. Nothing was bruised but my ego, since by now everyone was quite entertained by my talent for breaking chairs, and the jokes had started in earnest. I laughed along with them. But with the second chair breaking, Leilani decided that she had had enough. She sat down elsewhere and announced, "I don't want to sit on your lap anymore, Daddy!"

To this day, every time I see that type of chair, I think twice before sitting on it! It takes a lot of faith to sit on a chair that broke not once – but twice! What are the odds of breaking two chairs in one night? How do you ever look those people in the eyes again? I'm still getting teased about it to this day! Thankfully, I caught Leilani both times. She was never hurt and she never hit the ground. She was safely cradled in my arms. But her faith in Daddy was somewhat shaken after the second chair broke.

· · · · ·

Faith is a funny thing. Sometimes you don't know how strong it really is until it's all you have left. The writer of the book of Hebrews describes faith in this way: **"Faith is being sure of what we hope for and certain of what we do not see."** (Hebrews 11:1; NIV 1984) While we walk upon this earth, we can't see God – at least not in the way that we want to see Him. But part of this idea of childlike faith is just crawling up on His lap and trusting that He will never let you fall. Yes, there will be times when you will hear that "cracking sound," and you might even feel like you're starting to fall. But faith is knowing that no matter what happens in this life, Jesus is right there with us, and even when the chair breaks and we are headed for the ground, He will catch us and hold us tightly in His arms.

Pray about It

Dear Father,
   Thank You for always being there. In a world that is always unexpectedly changing, I know You are consistent. Keep my faith strong in the times when I feel as though life is falling apart beneath me. Remind me that You will always

uphold me and will never let me fall. In Jesus' name I pray, Amen.

Talk about It

- Think of a time in your life when you felt as if you were falling, and yet all the while, God was holding onto you tightly. Looking back on this experience, how do you think it has changed your relationship with God?

- Why do you think God wants us to trust Him even in the things we cannot see? Do you think this difficult to do?

Live It Out

Designate a favorite, comfortable chair in the house as your "thankfulness chair." Every time you happen to sit down on this chair, make it a habit to remind yourself of one thing that God has done in your life to bless you and strengthen your faith. Try to think of something different every time.

The Gold Medal

"The workers who were hired about five in the afternoon came and each received a denarius. So when those came who were hired first, they expected to receive more. But each one of them also received a denarius. When they received it, they began to grumble against the landowner. 'These who were hired last worked only one hour,' they said, 'and you have made them equal to us who have borne the burden of the work and the heat of the day.' But he answered one of them, 'I am not being unfair to you, friend. Didn't you agree to work for a denarius? Take your pay and go. I want to give the one who was hired last the same as I gave you. Don't I have the right to do what I want with my own money? Or are you envious because I am generous?' So the last will be first, and the first will be last." (Matthew 20:9-16)

When Maile was three years old and Leilani was just 18 months, Christy decided that she wanted to do a 5K Fun Run. We thought it would be an enjoyable activity for us to do as a family. Christy could sprint far ahead of me (I have to confess that I really don't believe in running for fun) and I would jog along at a slow, leisurely pace with Maile beside me, and Leilani in a baby pack strapped to my back.

Right before the race began, an announcement was made that the first 100 racers across the finish line would receive gold medals. I looked around at the 300 or so people who would be racing against me, and suddenly my competitive juices kicked in. I decided that I was going to get a medal!

With a gunshot, the race started – and seemingly only five steps into the race Maile called out: "Daddy, I'm tired! Can you carry me?" I couldn't believe it. But yes, of course I agreed to carry her. So now I had Leilani on my back and was holding Maile in front, and I was still determined to get that medal!

The look on the faces of all the people who were getting left in the dust by a guy carrying two kids was absolutely priceless. Every once in a while, I'd ask Maile if she wanted to try running again. And after thinking about it for a few seconds, she would politely reply: "No thanks." Oh well – at least I tried!

Of course, the high temperature on this day also happened to be record-breaking. Not a cloud in the sky as the temperature passed 100 degrees. The finish line seemed to be a thousand miles away. Sweat was constantly running into my eyes and stinging them. And carrying all the extra weight sure wasn't helping. With every step, I felt new blisters forming and sweat dripping off of me. At one point near the end, Maile even felt the need to tell me: "Daddy, you're getting really sweaty!" (As if I didn't know!)

It reached the point where I started to wonder whether or not I was really going to make it – and if I didn't make it, how would my kids ever explain this story in the future? I had played football, basketball, and baseball in high school, plus some basketball in college. I don't recall my legs, feet, and back ever hurting so much!

But I am proud to say that we made it all the way through the race! It was brutal, but we did it. And when I crossed that finish line, holding my two children, the gal in charge of bestowing the medals on the "winners" gave me a medal – and then she placed medals around the necks of Leilani and Maile as well. What?? The girls were thrilled with their reward, and proudly showed off their medals to Mommy and everyone they met at the finish line. I was a bit confused. I had done all the hard work, and yet we all received the exact same reward. Even Maile, who took barely five steps of the 5K, and Leilani, who took exactly zero steps, each got a medal! (Hey, maybe next time, someone can carry ME!)

. . . . .

This incident reminds me of the parable that Jesus told about a boss who was hiring workers for his vineyard. You can find this parable in Matthew 20:1-16. The basic story is that the boss goes out first thing in the morning to find some workers, and promises each of them one coin for a day's work. The boss goes out several times throughout the day to gather more workers, and he promises each of them one coin for their labor, even though they started later in the day. He even promises the last group of workers one coin each, and they only worked for an hour!

At the end of the day, when it was time to pay the laborers, the workers who had toiled the entire day each received their one coin – and then became upset because those who had only worked for an hour received the same payment. The reward was the same, regardless of the amount of effort. They confronted the boss about how seemingly unfair this was to those who had labored all day in the hot sun. But he reminded them that he had promised them one coin from the beginning, and they had agreed. As the boss, he could do whatever he wanted with his money.

So here's the main point of this parable. It's easy for us to focus on injustices in the world, and to complain about the world not being fair. But do we really want life to be "fair?" Do we want to be given what we *really* deserve? God is perfect and pure. We are sinful and unclean. God is just, and the wages of sin is death – which we ALL deserve. Yet God gives eternal life to *all* who believe in Jesus as Lord and Savior! Both the lifelong Christian and the last-minute convert will be spending their eternal lives with Jesus.

When we focus on the world's view of fairness, we're exposing our selfishness. Instead, we should think about who can we strap to our back – and hold in our arms – to help them finish the race of faith (cf. 2 Timothy 4:7). It's God's grace after all; He can do what He wants with it. What a blessing that He's given it to you!

Pray about It

Dear Father,

Give me strength to remain constant in my faith and to guide and comfort others who may be struggling. Keep my focus on the rewards of this life, not just the injustices. I know I have never done anything to deserve eternal life, and yet through faith in Your Son Jesus who died for my sins, I know that I will receive that incredible blessing. Thank You for giving me so much more than I deserve! In Jesus' name, Amen!

Talk about It

- It is easy to get caught up in the world's view of fairness. What are some ways in which God's sense of justice is completely different from that of the world?

- Are there people in your life who need a break from judgment and could use a demonstration of God's unearned acceptance?

Live It Out

How can you help someone finish the race? As a family, think of one person you can encourage in their faith this week and help them along toward the finish line. Think of a few thoughtful, personal ways that you can help guide and support them in the faith.

Thanks for joining me on the adventure of childlike faith! I'd love to hear from you! E-mail me your Abba Daddy (or Mommy) Do stories to: jacobyoumans@gmail.com. I'm praying for you!

Mailing Address:
Dr. Jacob Youmans
Director, DCE Program
Associate Professor of Education
Concordia-Texas
11400 Concordia University Drive
Austin, TX 78726

Also from Tri-Pillar Publishing

Talking Pictures: How to Turn a Trip to the Movies Into a Mission Trip
Dr. Jacob Youmans

Powerful Love: An Introduction to Christianity
Rev. Dr. Lloyd Strelow

Extraordinary News for Ordinary People
Rev. Heath Trampe

Breaking Barriers: Realizing Spiritual Victory Through Christian Martial Arts
Rev. J. Brown

www.tripillarpublishing.com